Growing Successful orchids

in the Greenhouse and Conservatory

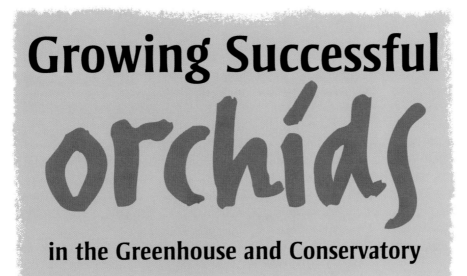

Growing Successful orchids in the Greenhouse and Conservatory

GUILD OF MASTER CRAFTSMAN
PUBLICATIONS LTD

First published 2003 by
Guild of Master Craftsman Publications Ltd,
166 High Street, Lewes,
East Sussex BN7 1XU

Reprinted 2003

ISBN 1 86108 271 1

British Cataloguing in Publication Data
A catalogue record of this book is available from the British Library.

Book design by Andy Harrison

Typefaces: Caslon 224 Book and Strayhorn

Colour origination by Viscan Graphics, Singapore

Printed and bound by Kyodo Printing, Singapore

Contents

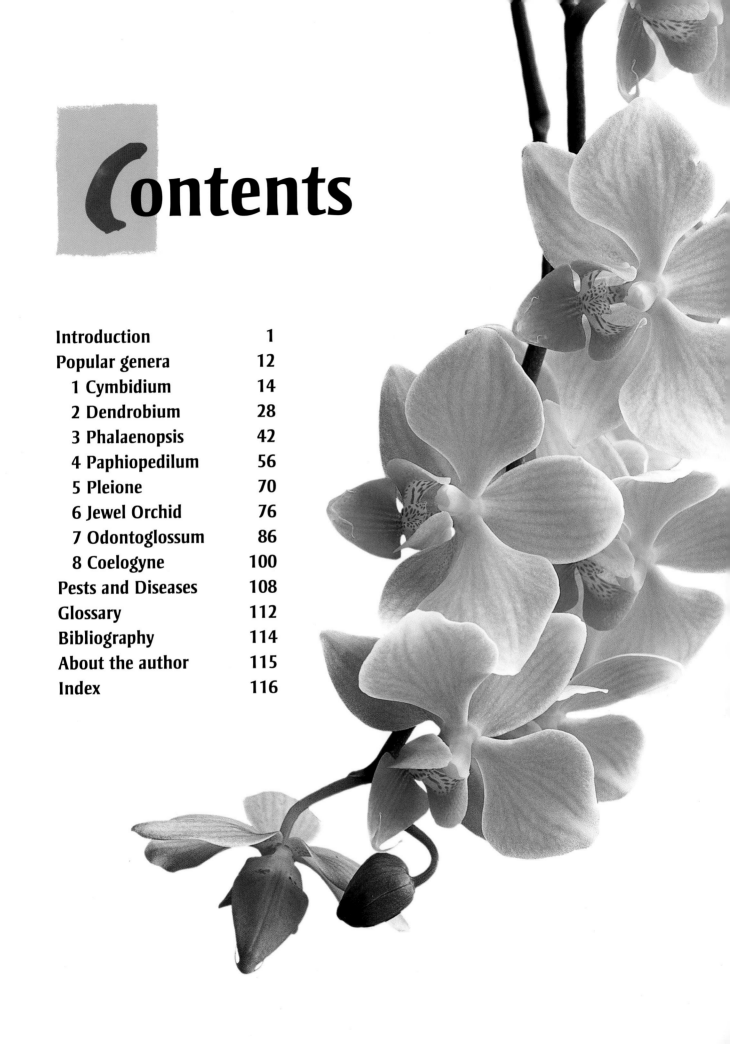

introduction

The Orchid Family (Orchidaceae) is the largest and most varied of all the flowering families and has, without doubt, caused more problems worldwide than any other. People have been fined and jailed for trading illegally in rare, expensive orchids; have had orchids confiscated; and have even died attempting to obtain these exquisite wonders of nature. These mysterious, magical and sophisticated plants are very seductive, sometimes dangerously so.

Their attraction lies in their seemingly endless varieties, colours and shapes, their exceptional beauty, and the fact that many resemble bees, wasps, butterflies and even spiders to attract their corresponding pollinator. They come in a wide range of sizes: at just 4mm (5/32in) high, the smallest plant would be lost inside a thimble, while the largest reaches over 30 metres (100ft). Several are fragrantly scented, but many produce

ABOVE *Bulbophyllum leopardinum*: exudes a strong odour of rotting meat

RIGHT *Ophrys apifera*, also known as the Bee Orchid for its striking resemblance to the insect

LEFT *Dendrobium* 'Sailor Boy': a sympodial, multi-stemmed orchid

ABOVE *Dendrobium victoria-reginae* **BELOW** *Oncidium flexuosum*

a very unpleasant smell, such as *Bulbophyllum leopardinum*, which exudes a strong odour of rotting meat, likely to attract flies for pollination (see page 1).

Origins – in myth and fact

A rather charming story from Western Java recounts how orchids arrived on earth. According to the tale, a beautiful, virtuous and generous goddess, named Dewi Ratna Sastrawati, came down to earth to teach goodness and understanding. Spurned by the people, Dewi was driven into the forest. During her flight, the goddess dropped her scarf, which was blown from tree to tree and wherever the scarf landed a beautiful, tender orchid grew. A romantic story, but of course the facts are very different.

Millions of years ago, when dinosaurs roamed the earth, among the flowering plants that were evolving was the orchid. Today, much of that plant life has disappeared, but the orchid family has gone from strength to strength. There are over 25,000 **species** worldwide, which cover just about every country on the globe, with the exception of the frozen and arid regions. Some will mainly be found in the tropics, such as dendrobium (see facing page) and vanda which are endemic to Asia and Australasia, and maxillaria, oncidium (see facing page) and laelia which are specific to the Americas; but others, like habenaria (see top right) and spiranthes (see bottom right), occur throughout the world.

Orchid history

The history behind orchids is as fascinating and exotic as the orchids themselves. Orchids like *Bletilla striata* (see page 5) were first documented in Chinese manuscripts many years before the birth of Christ, and cultivated in the Orient long before the eighteenth century. It was the Chinese philosopher Confucius (551–479BC) who named the orchid 'lan' (Chinese for 'orchid') and attracted the Chinese people to these plants which, at the time, were mainly cymbidiums.

In Japan, orchids were also revered. The first written accounts appeared in the mid-seventeenth century when a German doctor, who worked for a Dutch Trading company, began recording the orchids that he had seen; and, in 1772, *Igansai-ranpin* was published, which described cymbidiums, dendrobiums and aerides.

Orchids in demand

In the early 1800s, professional plant hunters from Europe sailed to South America, risking their lives for the fortunes that were to be made on their return. Many succumbed to tropical diseases, while others had to cope with snakes, wild animals, hostile tribesmen and the heavy tropical rain and flooding. As competition grew from other hunters, so did jealousy, rivalry and corruption. Those who survived all this and managed to return with the plants became very wealthy, and were often immortalized in the names of the orchids they discovered. Indeed, the demand for orchids was so great at this time that Wilhelm Micholitz even sent back an orchid growing in a human skull, which was auctioned (as it was) for an enormous sum of money (see illustration on page 7).

Sadly, the hunters often devastated the natural orchid habitats, stripping entire forests of literally millions of orchids. It is said that 4,000 trees were cut down to reach the orchids growing on them. And one man alone is reputed to have sent around 100,000 plants to England. Unfortunately,

ABOVE *Habenaria dentata* **BELOW** *Spiranthes amoena*: habenaria and spiranthes may be found growing throughout the world, except in the frozen and arid regions

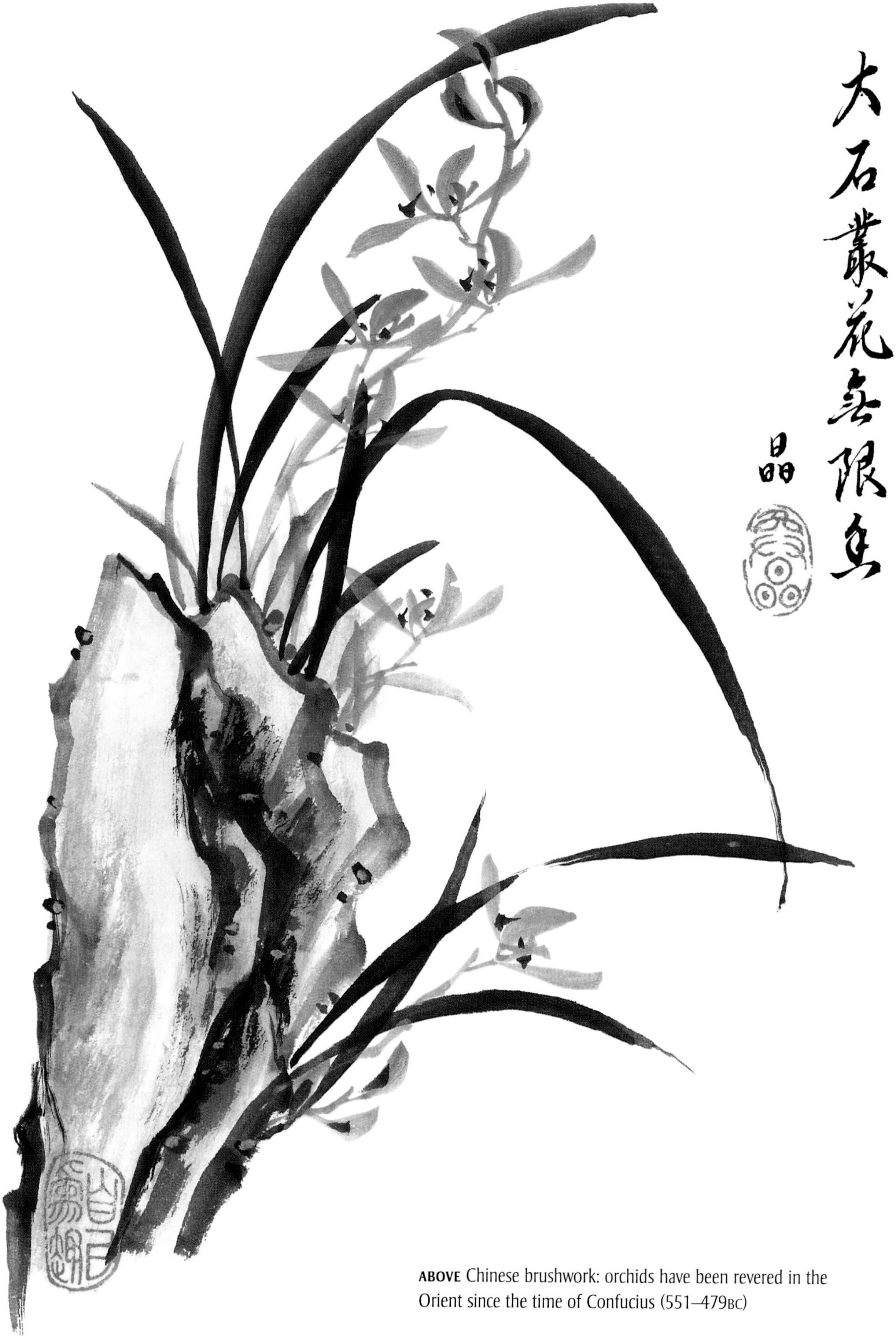

ABOVE Chinese brushwork: orchids have been revered in the Orient since the time of Confucius (551–479BC)

ABOVE Orchids such as *Bletilla striata* were documented in Chinese manuscripts long before the birth of Christ

many of the plants did not survive the long journey home, and those that did were often placed in the wrong (and sometimes very hostile) conditions and they, too, succumbed.

In modern times, the beauty of orchids has also captured the imagination of philatelists, both in the design of stamps and in their collection. There is hardly a country in the world that has not issued a set of stamps that include an orchid or a selection of orchids. Every single popular genus has been depicted, as well as obscure and little known genera like ipsea (a **monotypic** genus confined to Sri Lanka), caleana (a rare Australian genus), arethusa (a small terrestrial genus from the USA), mystacidium (mainly from South Africa) and many, many more.

Medicinal

Orchids have not been noted only for their beauty, though. The earliest report on 'orchis' plants is said to have been in 370–285BC by the Greek philosopher Theophrastus, who observed that the pseudobulbs resembled male testicles and therefore named the plant 'orchis' (the Greek word for 'testicles').

Many years later, in the first century AD, a Greek physician named Dioscorides wrote *De Materia Medica* in which he described hundreds of plants, including two orchids that he claimed were sexual stimulants because of the shape of their **pseudobulbs**. This theory continued to evolve until, eventually, the ancient Greeks believed that eating the pseudobulbs and roots could provoke Aphrodite (Goddess of Love) and also influence the sex of an unborn child.

Belief in the power of the orchid was maintained over centuries. In 1640, John Parkinson wrote in *Theatrum Botanicum*: 'if a man ate a large orchid tuber, he would beget many children.' And in William Shakespeare's play *Hamlet*, a garland made of 'long purples', that was probably *Orchis mascula* (Early Purple Orchid, see page 6), which had a reputation for having aphrodisiac qualities, was mentioned as being worn by Ophelia.

During Shakespeare's time and up to the nineteenth century, *Orchis mascula* tubers were collected, dried, and made into a milky drink, similar to the popular Turkish drink 'salep'. It is still used today as a medicinal drink for patients

ABOVE *Orchis mascula* (Early Purple): the tubers have been used in a medicinal drink for many years

ABOVE *Vanilla fragrans*: popular with the ancient Aztecs, who used to drink vanilla mixed with chocolate, as they believed it increased their strength

because it is full of minerals and easy on the stomach. However, as with all wild orchids the world over, it is illegal to remove *Orchis mascula* from its habitat; but, despite this, the drink has become a major export and is now endandering these orchids.

In many cultures today, orchids are considered a remedy for various ailments. For instance, in China, orchids are used as a medicine for complaints such as stomachache; and in Malaya it is said that the bulbs of *Nervilia aragoana* when boiled help sickness after childbirth. In Malacca there is an orchid that is supposed to be good for boils; and in the West Indies it is believed that the liquid of the boiled bulbs of *Bletia purpurea* cure fish poisoning. In addition, there is an orchid in Chile that is supposed to be a very good diuretic.

In spite of the popularity of orchids today, there are still many people who are unaware that vanilla is an orchid – and one with a story too: the Aztecs of Mexico drank vanilla mixed in chocolate, as they thought it promoted great strength (see above).

In 1753, the botanist Linnaeus wrote in *Materia Medica* that he recommended vanilla as an aphrodisiac. Prior to that, the well-known English pirate and botanist William Dampier, who captured and plundered a great many ships,

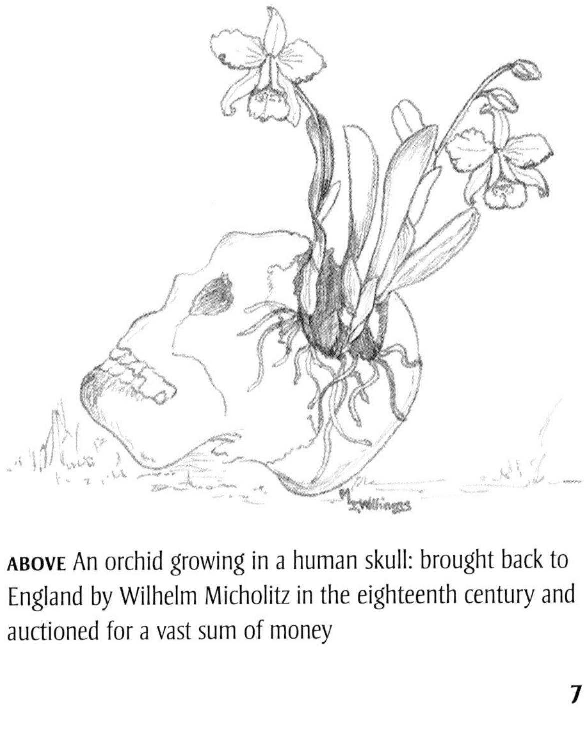

ABOVE An orchid growing in a human skull: brought back to England by Wilhelm Micholitz in the eighteenth century and auctioned for a vast sum of money

Characteristics of different orchid genera

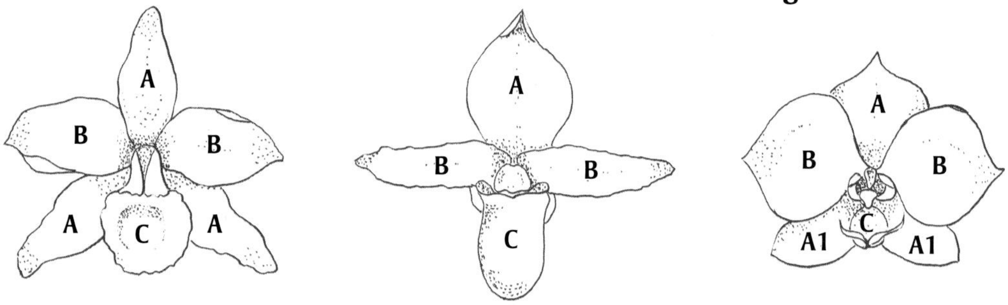

Dendrobium   Paphiopedilum   Phalaenopsis

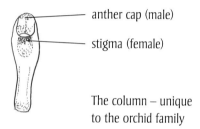

A – dorsal sepal
A1 – lateral sepals
B – petals
C – lip or labellum

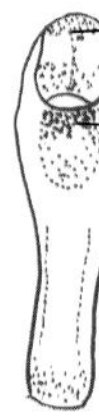

The column – unique to the orchid family

wrote: 'Our privateers have often thrown (vanilla) away when they took any, wondering why the Spaniards should lay up 'tobacco' stems.'

It took some time before westerners recognized and appreciated the value and flavour of vanilla, but now the essence and seed pods are readily available in most supermarkets.

Anatomy

It is not within the scope of this book to detail the anatomy of the orchid, but it is interesting to note that the orchid is the only flower that has the **stamen** (male) and **stigma** (female) united into one structure, known as the **column**. It is this feature that identifies the flower as an orchid (see illustration on left).

Growth patterns

The orchid family has two growth patterns: **monopodial** and **sympodial**. Simply speaking, monopodial orchids produce one stem that grows in one direction and lengthens year by year. The plants normally produce many **aerial roots**, which will either attach themselves to any possible surface available, or hang in the air to collect moisture (see illustration below). The **inflorescence** appears from a leaf **axil** or opposite a leaf axil, and the plants do not possess storage organs for food or water, as they are generally found in tropical countries, where rain is an everyday occurrence.

The vanda is a very good example of a monopodial orchid, with leaves that are arranged in two opposite and alternating rows along the main stem. Other monopodial orchids include

Monopodial

Phalaenopsis   Vanda   Aerides

ABOVE Orchids in their natural habitat: growing high on tree branches

aerides, phalaenopsis, ascocendas, renantheras, angraecums, luisia and aerangis.

The majority of orchids, however, are sympodial and multi-stemmed (see illustration below). They are able to store food in pseudobulbs and regulate their water supply during the dry, resting periods. In subtropical countries, these pseudobulbs swell to enormous sizes in preparation for the dry season, but in tropical areas they develop very little, as water storage is not so essential. At the end of the season the plant ceases growth, until the following year when it begins again, as with, for example, dendrobium, cattleya, masdevallia, ansellia and pholidota.

Habitat

Orchids grow on trees (**epiphyte**), on rocks (**lithophyte**), in the ground (**terrestrial**) and even underground (**saprophyte**). Their adaptability is probably one of the reasons for their long survival. But although they attach themselves to trees and other plants, they are not parasitic, as is often thought: parasites rely

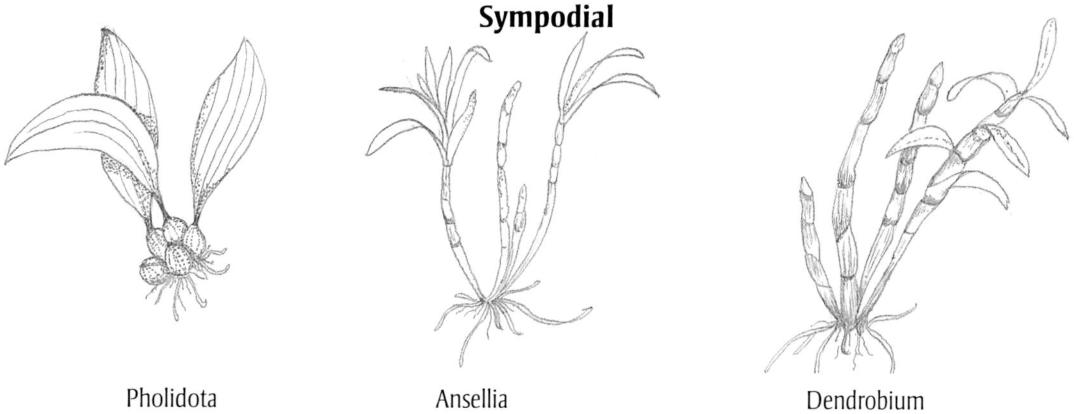

ABOVE *Paphiopedilum* Anja x Diversion **BELOW** *Cymbidium* Ann Green x Pink Ice: hybrids come in a magnificent array of colours, shapes and sizes

RIGHT *Coelogyne cristata* growing on rocks

on their host for food – orchids use their host purely for support.

Hybrids

Unknown to many orchid enthusiasts, most of the **hybrids** seen today originate from species that are still found growing in China, the Philippines, Thailand, Malaysia, South Africa and Central and South America, though due to ruthless collectors some have become extremely rare.

Yearly, many hybrids are added and, to date, no other flowering plant has given birth to so many hybrids, some which involve as many as five crosses. The blooms appear in every shape, size and colour imaginable and, with care, some will flower for up to three months.

About this book

This book is an introduction to the origins and care of some of the most popular orchids grown today. The myth that orchids are exclusive to the wealthy (as they were in the eighteenth century), and almost impossible to grow because they are delicate and need hothouse conditions, has certainly been dispelled, as more and more garden enthusiasts turn their attention to these beauties.

Tropical conditions are not always needed to grow orchids successfully: this book describes

those suitable for cooler climates, as well as those that are easy to cultivate in your home. Just remember that if you have some knowledge of the habitat, temperatures, altitude and country of origin where orchid species thrive, you are halfway towards knowing how to look after them. For instance, a cymbidium from the cold Himalayan region is unlikely to appreciate a hot, steamy glasshouse with temperatures of 30°C (83°F) and, equally, a phalaenopsis from the tropical jungles will not take well to extremely cold night temperatures of 7°C (45°F) or less. So, before spending a lot of money and then discovering that you are unable to give them the environment they require, look into the various types of orchids and see what it is they need; then decide whether you are able to provide for those needs.

On a final note, you will see that I have not referred to any particular brands of insecticide, pesticide or fungicide throughout this book. This is because the chemical names, properties and their permitted uses are constantly changing; it would therefore be unwise of me to recommend brands that are available today but may not be tomorrow. I therefore strongly recommend that you always seek expert advice from a specialist orchid nursery.

Popular genera

Cymbidium

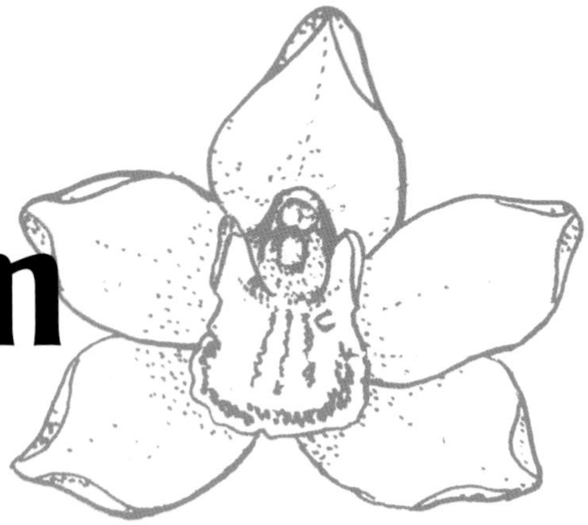

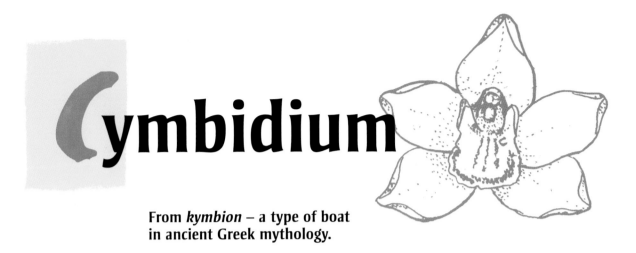

From *kymbion* – a type of boat in ancient Greek mythology.

This large genus of approximately 300 terrestrial and epiphytic species is found in both hemispheres, though predominantly in Asia. Forty-nine species occur in eight provinces of China, and other species occur in Madagascar, India, Myanmar, Sri Lanka, Malaysia, the Philippines, Japan and Australia.

ABOVE *C. ensifolium*: noted in manuscripts during the Chin Dynasty (221–202BC) for its medicinal qualities

LEFT *C. bursundian* 'Sydney'

History

It is interesting to note that cymbidium is probably the oldest recorded orchid in the world. The great Chinese philosopher Confucius (551–479BC) referred to it as the 'king of fragrant flowers', and many ancient poems and paintings make reference to it. The earliest Chinese manuscript given entirely to botany was written during the Chin Dynasty (221–202BC). In this manuscript, *Cymbidium ensifolium* (left) is discussed under the herbal section, as the thickened root, when boiled in water and mixed with fermented glutinous rice, was said to be good for curing stomachache.

Popularity

Dr John Fothergill was the first European to take *Cymbidium ensifolium* back to the west after collecting it in China in 1778. However, cymbidium species that remain popular in China and Japan are now not as widely grown in the west. One species in particular that is much prized by the Chinese is *Cymbidium sinense*, as it normally flowers around the Lunar New Year and has beautifully scented flowers of a deep brown-red colour.

Generally speaking, though, cymbidiums are still one of the most popular orchids cultivated today, and possibly the most widely grown, both as potted plants and for the cut-flower market, because of the ease with which they are able to adapt to their surroundings: they do well in temperate and subtropical climates; make ideal plants for garden rooms and conservatories; and may be kept outdoors in early summer.

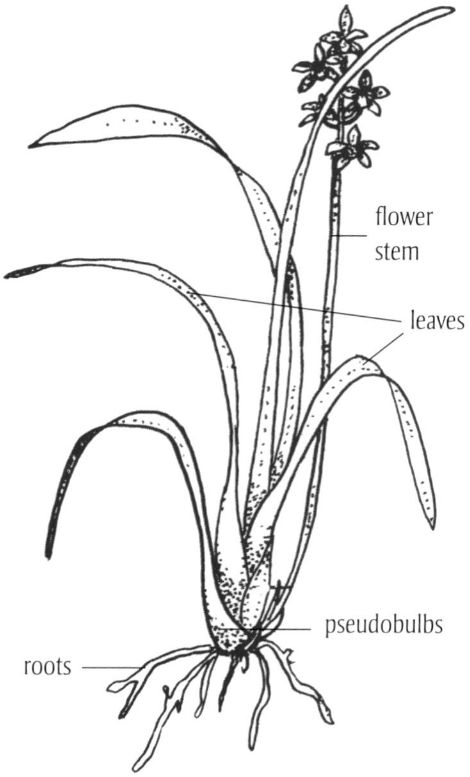

ABOVE The characteristic features of cymbidiums

Characteristics

The pseudobulbs of cymbidiums may be small or large, often elongated, and covered in the sheathing bases of the overlapping leaves (see illustration on left). The leaves are normally long, narrow, erect or **pendent**, with either a thick or thin texture, and the pendulous or erect inflorescence that appears from the base of a pseudobulb has medium to large flowers that are usually sweet-smelling. The petals and **sepals** are widely spreading and free, and there are two pollinia. The **trilobate lip** has erect side **lobes** closely embracing the column, with several **lamellae** on the **disc**.

Hybrids

Although cymbidiums have been grown for thousands of years, it was not until the mid-1800s that the first hybrid was registered. It was given the name *C. eburneum-lowianum* (*C. eburneum* x *C. lowianum*, see below).

With its large, white, fragrant flowers, *C. eburneum* (see facing page and page 18), which comes from North India where it grows at elevations of 1,515m (5,000ft), was soon recognized as having potential for hybridizing.

ABOVE *C. eburneum-lowianum*: the first hybrid, registered in the mid-1800s

ABOVE *C. eburneum*

ABOVE *C. eburneum*: becoming increasingly rare due to its popularity in hybridizing

RIGHT *C. lowianum*: used as a partner to *C. eburneum* to create the first cymbidium hybrid

But despite the fact it was once available in large numbers, its role in hybridizing has, unfortunately, resulted in it becoming quite scarce.

C. lowianum (right), from Myanmar, was chosen as the partner to *C. eburneum* in this first cross – and no wonder, with its handsome sprays of hugely attractive, apple-green flowers (not to be confused with *C. giganteum*).

C. eburneum-lowianum was followed later by a further 14 hybrids, but most of them, with the exception of this one, were primarily of botanical interest.

Species that have been used extensively around the world to hybridize the cool-loving cymbidiums include: *C. eburneum*, *C. lowianum*, *C. ensifolium*, *C. grandiflorum* (see page 20), *C. tigrinum*, *C. erythrostylum*, *C. insigne* (see page 20), *C. pumilum*, *C. tracyanum* (see pages 22–23), and *C. devonianum*. These species are found growing wild over a wide range, from the Himalayas to the coast of China and as far south as Australia. However, most of the cool-loving hybrids widely grown today have been bred from species in the Himalayas; species native to other areas have mostly been used to cultivate the miniature varieties.

The modern hybrids you see today in garden centres or orchid nurseries are the result of years of crossing and recrossing by humans. The plants are robust, with large, oval pseudobulbs and long, straplike leaves, and the flowers are exquisite, appearing in just about every colour (including green, see page 24) and combination possible. Healthy, well-tended plants can develop as many as ten **spikes** at a time, and mature plants are easy to grow and bring into flower, provided a few simple requirements are met.

Conditions required for cultivation

Even during the winter months, cymbidiums continue to grow, albeit very slowly, so it is essential to keep the potting mix just moist. They must also have sufficient filtered or dappled light, one of the most important factors affecting flower production, together with a substantial drop in night temperature during the summer to initiate the formation of flower spikes. From the end of

the summer through to autumn and winter, cymbidiums need to receive as much bright light as possible.

During the winter, when the plants are inside (be it the house or greenhouse), a comfortable daytime temperature of around 15–18°C (59–65°F) is quite adequate. Night temperatures of 10°C (50°F) should be maintained throughout the autumn, winter and spring months, but may be allowed to drop safely to 7°C (45°F) if the outside temperature drops below freezing. What is important, though, is that the night temperature should not be allowed to rise above 14°C (58°F) when the flower spikes have appeared, as this can cause premature bud drop.

During the summer months, temperatures should ideally be kept below 29°C (85°F), but this may sometimes be difficult. If the plants are in a greenhouse, the ventilators should be open, but make sure the plants are not in a draught. If the plants are in the house, place them outside in dappled shade under a pergola or on a shady patio, but never in direct burning sun.

If heating is used to maintain the temperature level, or if the summer is hot, plants will benefit greatly by **damping down** a couple of times a day, particularly first thing in the morning.

Once the blooms appear, make sure that the humidity level is kept down, otherwise the flowers will very quickly become spotted and unsightly.

Potting mix

Throughout the world, growers have experimented with various types of material in which to grow cymbidiums, but really there is no single mix that is believed to be the best. In the

Cymbidium species that have been frequently used for hybridizing include *C. grandiflorum* (**ABOVE**) and *C. insigne* (**BELOW**)

early days of cultivating cymbidiums, a mix of peat moss, sand and leaf litter was used. However, a suggested suitable compost would be a mix of pine bark (about 45%), coarse washed sand, peat moss (approx. 40%), perlite, a handful of charcoal (10%) and polystyrene chunks in the bottom. There are no hard and fast rules about the proportions of each – just experiment and see what suits your needs. If you are not happy about doing this, you can always buy a special orchid mix from a nursery.

One thing to note with cymbidiums is that they are slightly acid-loving. The pH of the mix needs to be around 5.5–6.0 (a pH meter will give you the readings); the acidity may be adjusted by adding dolomite and limestone. With the gradual breakdown of bark and peat, the alkalinity of the potting mix will rise. If this persists, repot the plant in fresh potting mix.

Watering and feeding

a) Water

Cymbidiums, like most plants, need more water during their growing season (spring, summer and early autumn) than they do during late autumn and winter. It is always a difficult subject to approach but, generally speaking, it is safer to underwater than to overwater. The role of the pseudobulb in nature is actually to store water in preparation for long, dry periods that may occur; therefore, enough water must be given to keep these pseudobulbs green and smooth. If they begin to look shrivelled and pale, the plant is stressed and lacks water.

There are several conditions that dictate how much and how often to water:

1) the weather
2) the potting mix
3) natural rainfall

1) If the weather is hot and dry with a high temperature range of 23–27°C (73–80°F), plants will require water every other day. Lower temperatures constitute a watering every third day. With temperatures of 20°C (68°F) or lower, once a week is sufficient. If the compost is very dry, give the plants a really good soaking by standing their pots in a bucket of water.

2) The type of potting mix will have a great influence on watering requirements. If the mix is very open (coarse bark, etc.), watering will need to be heavier and more frequent, otherwise most of the water will run straight through with very little being retained for the plant. A finer mix will retain a great deal more water and therefore requires less. Use common sense – no hard and fast rule can be laid down when each day or week could produce varying conditions.

3) If the plant is outside in the summer but protected from the rain (on a covered patio) and gets plenty of air circulation, it will need regular watering (as above). If, however, it is open to the elements and there are several days of rain, then obviously watering is unnecessary. But, a word of advice – when your plant is in full bloom it is wise to keep it undercover if you want the flowers to last as long as possible.

b) Feed

In the early days of orchid growing, fertilizers were considered unnecessary. This has changed today because of the type of compost used, and orchids certainly do need feeding in order to get the best out of them. It is worth remembering, though, that plants do not rely completely on the fertilizers we give them, as all healthy plants produce their own food through photosynthesis.

There are many specialist orchid fertilizers on the market, but a normal well-balanced plant food will do just as well. Check the proportions of the ingredients on the packet which should be labelled NPK, followed by numbers (e.g. NPK 10:10:10: (10% nitrogen (N), 10% phosphorus (P) and 10% potassium (K)). These figures can vary considerably depending on the type of plant fertilizer. Quite simply, nitrogen promotes the growth of the leaves, phosphorus the growth of flowers and stems, and potassium general plant vigour; thus, a fertilizer with the ratio of 30:10:10 is obviously high in nitrogen, and therefore suitable for the active growing period from spring to late summer. During the blooming period (usually late spring, but summer for some orchids), a blossom booster of 10:30:20 will help to promote good, healthy blooms.

Cymbidiums are gross feeders. So, in order for you to achieve the best results possible, I recommend you fertilize your plants weekly, rather than monthly, during their growing period. It is far better to give a weak solution

ABOVE *C.* Bodmin Moor 'Snow Drift'

frequently than to give a strong solution less often; plants will benefit greatly from this treatment. Remember, though, most orchid potting mixes have relatively few nutrients, so your cymbidium will rely on you to feed it well. In return, it will reward you with a fine show of flowers.

One last point: do not feed your cymbidium once it has started flowering – not only would it be a complete waste, but it would also enhance the breakdown of the potting mix, cause salt build-up and root injury.

Flower development

The appearance of the first flower spike is always an exciting time, and one that gives a great deal of pleasure and satisfaction. However, beginners sometimes find it difficult to distinguish the difference between a flower spike and new growth: the new growth is normally flat-looking and wider at

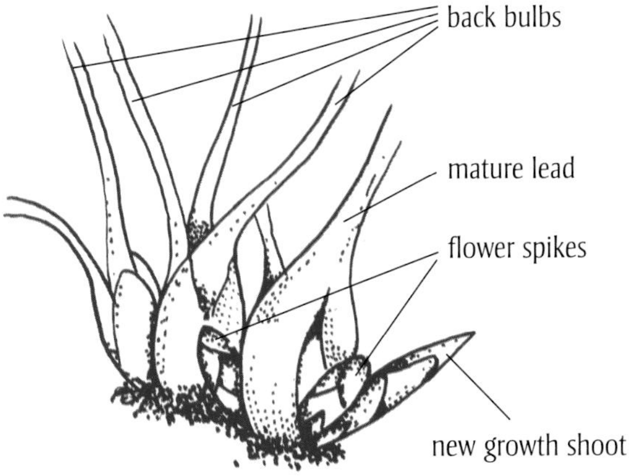

ABOVE New growth is normally flatter and wider at the base than the flower spike

ABOVE Tie the flower spikes to stakes as soon as possible

LEFT *C. tracyanum*

the base, compared to the flower spike, which tends to be much rounder (see illustration top right).

The spikes grow over a period of five to six weeks, during which time the buds gradually emerge from their protective sheaths. Some buds do not appear out of their sheaths until the spike is about 30cm (1ft) tall, while others may start to appear when the spike is only 5–6cm (2in) tall. Take great care not to accidentally knock the spike, as it will break off all too easily.

It is important to mark these flower spikes with a bamboo stake and, as the spikes grow, tie them to a stake, as shown in the illustration above. Without the support of a stake, the weight of the buds will pull the spike downwards. Not only will this spoil the look of the plant, it will also prevent the flowers from being seen at their best.

Under the correct care and conditions cymbidiums will produce several flowering stems that may last up to three months. During this time, the plant is using up most of its strength and resources, so it is wise to remove the flower spikes after they have been open for about six weeks. This gives the plant a chance to produce new growth for the following year, and you can enjoy the flower stems in a vase indoors. Of course, if the flowers begin to fade before the six weeks and look tired and spent, it would be advisable to remove them earlier.

No flowers?

Often, people who have either bought a beautiful flowering cymbidium or have received one as a gift will be heard to say: 'My plant hasn't flowered. What should I do?'

- First of all, look at the colour of the leaves. Are they a dark, lush green? If so, this may indicate that the plant needs more light.
- Are the leaves yellow? If so, this may indicate that they are lacking nitrogen – has the plant been given regular fertilizer?
- Is the plant actually growing? Growth can be stunted if there is a lack of magnesium, iron and nitrogen.
- Are the pseudobulbs shrivelled-looking? This will mean insufficient water or that the roots are in poor condition.
- Are they soft when pressed? This could be a fungal problem.
- How are the roots? If they are rotting, they will cause the potting mix to sour and should be removed.
- Is the pot full of weeds? Weeds will dehydrate a plant and should be removed by their roots completely.

Follow the guidelines carefully, as cymbidiums are happy to give their all if treated well.

ABOVE *C.* Caithness x *C.* Thurso: cymbidium hybrids exist in a spectacular range of colours, including green

Repotting

Cymbidiums should only be repotted when they have taken up all the available space in the pot (i.e. the **leading bulb** has reached the edge of the pot), or when the compost has turned sour. This must be done in early spring or when the plant has finished flowering.

If a healthy plant is to be **potted up**, it may be carefully lifted out of the old pot and placed into a new one. Fill the space around it with fresh potting mix and tap the pot a couple of times to ensure the mix packs down correctly.

Never **overpot** a plant: for instance, a 14cm (6in) potted plant should not be repotted into a 30cm (1ft) pot. Repot the plant step-by-step: putting it into a large pot is not going to make it grow larger. In fact, it could have the opposite affect and increase the risk of root rot.

When repotting because of poor compost, check the roots for signs of decay. If you do find any decayed roots, remove the old compost and trim them right back to the bulb with a clean, sterile pair of scissors or secateurs (see illustration below left). At the same time, cut away any dead pseudobulbs from the **rhizome**.

ABOVE Pot up step-by-step

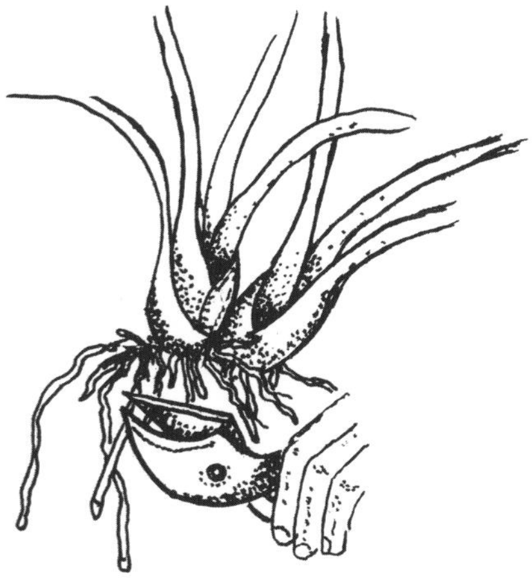

ABOVE Trim away dead roots

ABOVE Cut through the rhizome remove old bulbs

Propagation

If you want to increase your stock, **division** is the way to do it. Again, it must be done in early spring or after the plant has finished flowering.

First of all, you need a good mature plant that is ready to be potted up. Clear away the old potting mix, check the roots, and remove any old bulbs and dead flower spikes. Select at least four good bulbs on a rhizome; this may include two with no foliage and two with new growth. Then, using a sterile knife, cut through the rhizome and place them in fresh mix in a smaller pot (see illustration above).

Half-submerge the bulbs in the new potting mix to provide stability for the plant. This will help it to quickly establish a new rooting system. If the mother plant is large, several divisions may be made in the same way. But remember, this means there will be more plants of the same colour.

Healthy, single, leafless back bulbs may also be potted. Remove the old **husks** and roots and half-submerge the bulb in fresh potting mix in a small 10cm (4in) pot (see illustration on page 26). In a few weeks, a new plant will appear at the base of the bulb, though it will take at least four years to develop its first flowering stem. Do not remove the bulb – allow it to shrivel and die away naturally, even if it appears to be dead.

If the plant is to be placed in a greenhouse, make sure it has some shade. Alternatively, place the pot and bulb in a sealed polythene bag and hang it up either in the greenhouse or house. It will take anything up to eight weeks to produce a new lead

ABOVE Half-submerge a single back bulb

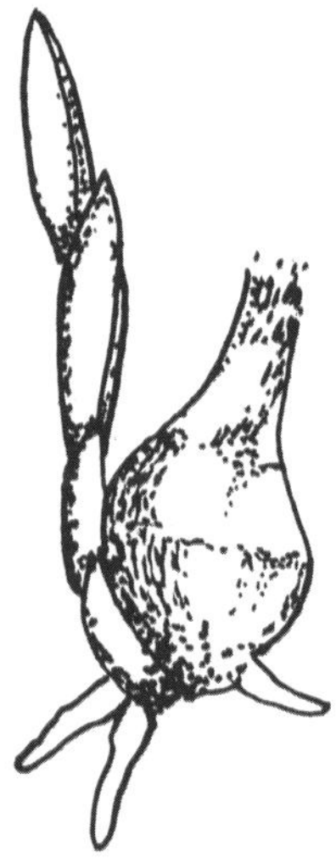

ABOVE Bulb and offshoot. A new lead will appear in approximately eight weeks

(see illustration above), at which time the pot should be removed from the bag and the plant should be treated as normal.

Pests and diseases

a) Pests

Fortunately, cymbidiums are not prone to many pests or fungal and bacterial diseases (unless plants are grown in poor conditions or an unsuitable environment). However, one little 'beastie' that will cause trouble if it is not discovered is the red spider mite, which is particularly fond of young plants. This pest feeds on the foliage by sucking the sap and producing a fine web on the underside of the leaves, causing a dry, silvery appearance.

Red spider mites are hardly visible to the naked eye, and are often not discovered until they have done considerable damage. Watch out for them, particularly when the weather is dry and hot. Look for their minute white eggs from the springtime and throughout the summer months. If there is a really bad infestation, you may have to resort to using a pesticide. However, do read the instructions carefully and take the necessary precautions if using one.

Biological control is the safest means. This may be done by introducing a predator that feeds on the red spider mite (a favourite is the ladybird). Predators may be introduced into your greenhouse if you have a number of plants, but prevention is always better than cure. So if you water your plants by hand, spray the underside of the foliage, as mites dislike water.

Aphids can also be a nuisance to cymbidiums – particularly when the buds appear, because the **pedicel** of the buds produces a sticky, sweet substance to which the aphids are attracted. Again, ladybirds will take care of these if introduced, but a quick solution of an insecticide (used with care) should do the trick. Alternatively, remove them by hand.

b) Diseases

When a plant is under stress and infected, it is more susceptible to fungal problems. Good culture, dry air and light conditions can help to prevent such problems occuring. Regular

ABOVE *C.* Forty-niner 'Alice Anderson'

checking of the foliage for early signs of fungal infections should be a part of your daily routine.

Two diseases will attack cymbidiums if they are in poor conditions: one is leaf-tip dieback; the other is a virus. Leaf-tip dieback is exactly that: the tip of the leaf begins to die, leaving a very ugly brown or black tip; it is a sign that something in the plant's culture is not quite up to par. It could be a draught, or it could be extremes in temperature change. Cut off the dead tip with a sterilized knife or scissors and spray with a proprietary systemic fungicide. Watch the plant for the next fortnight or so and if the leaves continue to produce this leaf-tip dieback, spray again with fungicide.

Virus is another matter. It is recognized by yellow-white streaks on the foliage that turn black as the leaf ages. Flowers will discolour soon after opening and, unfortunately, there is no known cure. In order to protect other plants, the infected plant *must* be burned and all tools used should be sterilized before being used on other plants. If you are unsure as to whether it is a virus, get expert advice before destroying the plant, as similar black markings can also appear through poor culture.

Bud drop is not necessarily caused by disease: it can be due to poor or unsuitable conditions, such as a lack of light indoors, temperatures too low, draughts, or over/underwatering. Before developing fully, the buds turn yellow and drop, or they develop to the point of opening and then drop.

Finally

If you would like to start a collection of cymbidiums and you think you have the correct facilities to grow them (cymbidiums make good houseplants), visit a specialist orchid nursery, or one that grows only cymbidiums, and seek expert advice on how to start your collection. Make sure the stock is good and robust: it would certainly be a waste of time and money if you were to start with a weak, infested plant, apart from the fact it would be disheartening to begin with a failure.

It is not necessary to buy the expensive plants, but it is necessary to choose well. And if you were to buy one which has its origins in *Cymbidium ensifolium*, you could have flowers for at least six months of the year, if not the whole year round.

ABOVE *C.* Jurassic Amber

dendrobium

From the Greek *dendron* (meaning 'tree') and *bios* (meaning 'life')

Founded by the famous botanist Olof Swartz in 1800, dendrobium is one of the largest genera, and also one of the most beautiful.

It has approximately 1,400 species and thousands of hybrids, which is perhaps due to its wide distribution from India, the Himalayas and Sri Lanka to China, Myanmar, Malaysia, Thailand, the Philippines, Japan, and southwards through Papua New Guinea, Australia and New Zealand in the Pacific region.

This means that dendrobiums are able to thrive in environments ranging from hot, steamy jungles to cold, exposed mountains. Many of them also live high up in the trees, hence their name, which is derived from the Greek *dendron*, meaning 'tree' and *bios*, meaning 'life'. It is therefore no wonder that the dendrobium has become so popular with amateur and professional orchid growers alike.

Characteristics

The flower form throughout the genus is fairly consistent, with the petals and sepals being equal, though the flowers vary considerably in size. In many species, the flowers will last up to nine months, provided pollination does not take place. And many have the most exotic scents, such as *D. heterocarpum* (syn. *D. aureum*) which is deliciously sweet, but not overpowering (see page 30), *D. primulinum*, *D. speciosum* (see page 30) and *D. superbum*.

The epiphytic sympodial stems are pseudobulbous, and either short and fleshy or elongated and resembling **canes** (see illustration below). These pseudobulbs store food and water to keep the plant supplied during the dry period; when the rain begins, so too does the new growth.

On the previous year's canes, flower buds in some species appear along the length of the stems from the **nodes**, transforming the lifeless canes into a profusion of colour when open. In others, large bunches of flowers on short stems burst forth from the upper nodes only, or long pendent

LEFT *D. transparens*

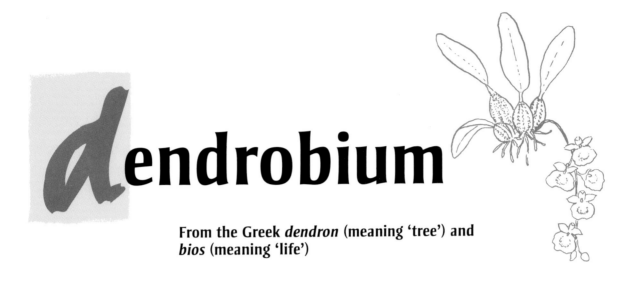

RIGHT *D. williamsonii*

ABOVE *D. densiflorum*: golden flowers appear along its pendent stems

ABOVE *D. heterocarpum*

RIGHT *D. speciosum*: both species have exotic scents

ABOVE *D. nobile*: once used extensively in hybridizing and a good species for beginners

flowering stems appear, densely covered in golden buds, as with, for example, *D. densiflorum* (see facing page and illustration below).

Types of dendrobium

The dendrobiums that are most easily cultivated are separated into two types: **evergreen** – from hot, humid, tropical rainforests, like New Guinea and Borneo, such as *D. phalaenopsis* (see illustration on page 33), and **deciduous** – from the fluctuating-climatic regions of Asia, such as *D. nobile* (above). The latter sheds its leaves after a year's growth and becomes dormant during the dry season.

Because the deciduous species and the hybrids from them require far less heat than the evergreen species and their hybrids (which need

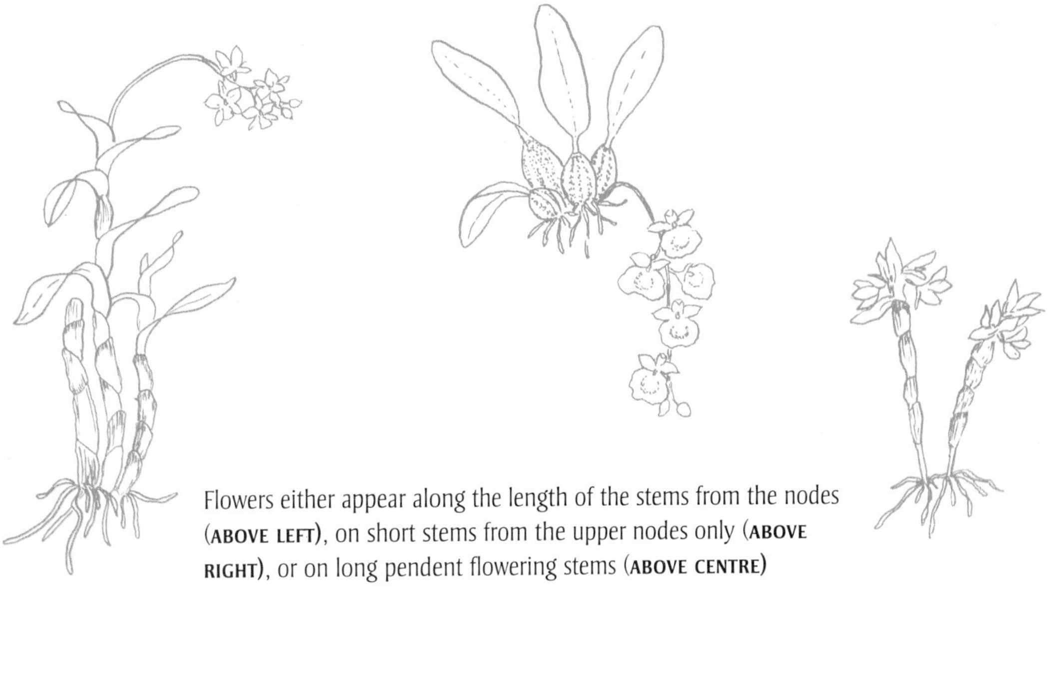

Flowers either appear along the length of the stems from the nodes (**ABOVE LEFT**), on short stems from the upper nodes only (**ABOVE RIGHT**), or on long pendent flowering stems (**ABOVE CENTRE**)

ABOVE *D. chrysotoxum*: a cool-loving species, frequently seen for sale

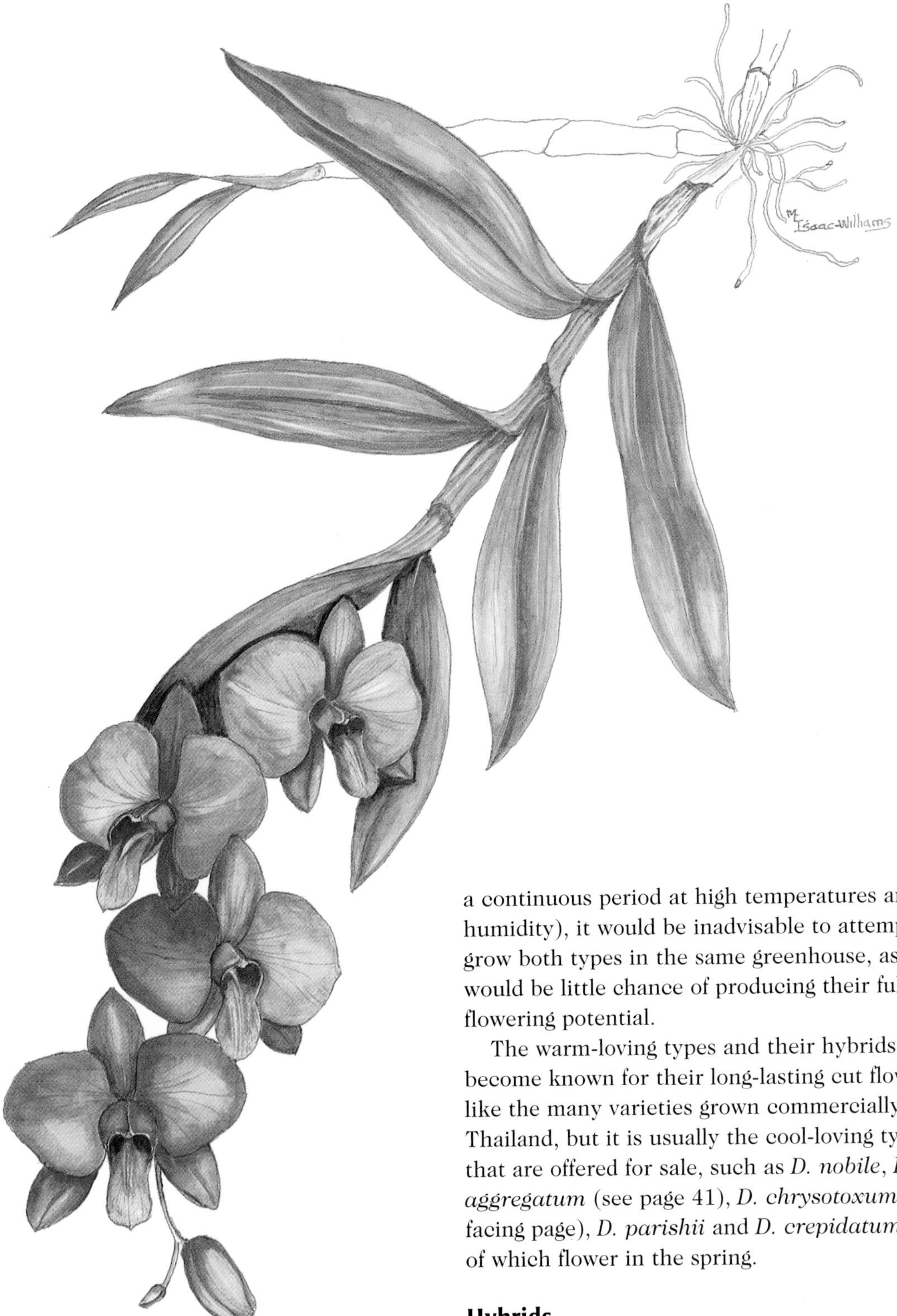

ABOVE *D. phalaenopsis*: a warm-loving Australian species

a continuous period at high temperatures and humidity), it would be inadvisable to attempt to grow both types in the same greenhouse, as there would be little chance of producing their full flowering potential.

The warm-loving types and their hybrids have become known for their long-lasting cut flowers, like the many varieties grown commercially in Thailand, but it is usually the cool-loving types that are offered for sale, such as *D. nobile*, *D. aggregatum* (see page 41), *D. chrysotoxum* (see facing page), *D. parishii* and *D. crepidatum* – all of which flower in the spring.

Hybrids

D. nobile, from India, was once used extensively in hybridizing: there are 77 hybrids registered in which it is a parent. It has large, 5cm (2in) flowers in rosy purple and white that appear on the long, canelike pseudobulbs of the previous

ABOVE *D. moniliforme*

year's growth, and has a rich maroon blotch on the **lip**. It first flowered in Britain in 1837, and has always been a readily available species. It is an easy, cool house orchid that blooms in the spring, and a good one for beginners.

More recently, the warm-loving Australian species *D. phalaenopsis* and the closely related

ABOVE *D. bigibbum* (Cooktown orchid): the state flower of Queensland, Australia

D. bigibbum or Cooktown orchid (below left), which is the state flower of Queensland, Australia, have become more popular in hybridizing. So far, there have been 266 hybrids registered with *D. phalaenopsis* as one parent, and *D. bigibbum* has been registered with 127 crosses. Both these plants may be found in the far northern tip of Australia, on the Cape York Peninsula, and are very attractive in their own right, with rich magenta flowers and deep, rich pink or pink-purple flowers respectively.

Conditions required for cultivation

During the summer, the cool and temperate varieties require a daytime temperature of between 15–20°C (59–68°F) and a night temperature of about 13°C (55°F). The warm types require 30°C (86°F) during daytime and about 20°C (68°F) at night.

Dendrobiums love high humidity during the summer months, so when the air temperature is high, spray the surrounding area to maintain the humidity. Make sure there is plenty of ventilation when increasing the humidity, though, as a

ABOVE *D. cariniferum*

humid, airless room or greenhouse is detrimental to plants. Also, remember that many dendrobiums live high up in the trees where there is always ventilation, so a period out in the garden during the summer would be beneficial; choose a very bright (but not sunny) position that is sheltered from the wind.

Late autumn, when the plants have finally completed their annual growth, is the time to move them into their winter home. Slowly reduce the watering and feeding over a period of four weeks, and then stop. As the days shorten, the deciduous types will react to the cooler temperatures and their leaves will begin to turn yellow and drop; this is quite natural and nothing to worry about. Even the evergreen plants may lose some leaves from the older canes, though they do not react as strongly as the deciduous types. The cool types will need approximately 13°C (55°F) during the day and about 10°C (50°F) at night. If you have the warm types, they will need daytime temperatures of 22°C (72°F) and 18°C (64°F) at night. Although *nobile* types are always kept warm in the summer months, they do need a lower temperature of approximately 10°C (50°F) during the autumn to encourage the formation of flowers, and both types must be given maximum light during the winter months. This means that if they are to stay in the house, they must be placed in a non-heated room, south-facing if possible, and prevented from coming into

ABOVE *D. pierardii*

ABOVE *D.* Utopia

contact with glass windowpanes, as this will cause damage to the plants if there is a frost outside. The same applies if the plants are to be housed in a greenhouse. Place them as near as possible to the light and keep them relatively dry.

Potting mix

The compost for dendrobiums should be loose but able to hold the plant securely in place; it must be able to absorb water easily, but at the same time drain well; and it is best if it is of a slightly acidic pH mix (refer to *Cymbidium*, page 20). Because of this, pine bark in medium chunks mixed with small pieces of charcoal and sphagnum moss makes a good medium – all are available at any orchid nursery or good garden centre. It is as simple as that. (Please note that normal flower compost is *not* suitable.)

Watering and feeding

a) Water

The cool, temperate, soft-caned species must go through the winter months with almost no water, as this is one of the key elements to being successful with flowering. If they are in a centrally heated house and the atmosphere is very dry, spray the roots once a month or give them a good single soak every eight weeks, but that is all. Remember, simulate nature: their natural habitat in Asia has cool, dry winters, with little or no rain.

By late winter, the canes may look shrivelled and dead, but as they begin their new growth and bud formation, water should be applied sparingly until good roots have formed. This will be the time to start a regular watering pattern.

To ensure water penetration after being semi-dry for several months, stand the pot in a bucket of water for about 15 minutes. Keep the compost moist throughout the summer and the canes will soon fatten up into lush, green stems. Spraying a fine mist will also benefit the plant, particularly during the hot, sunny spells.

The warm, hard-caned species usually require more water than the cool types. And even though they, too, need a winter rest, they must be kept moist throughout this period.

ABOVE *D. bracteosum*

ABOVE *D. formosum giganteum*

ABOVE *D. discolor*

b) Feed

Dendrobiums should be fed from early spring to early autumn on a fortnightly programme with a very weak solution of any high nitrogen formula, and during early autumn to mid-winter with a weak solution of a potash feed to ripen the canes. They should not be fed during the later winter months.

If you are a beginner and unsure of measurements, use a commercial orchid fertilizer diluted to half the normal strength. Spray the foliage with a fine mist of the solution, as well as applying it to the potting mix, but do make sure that it is very weak. It is not recommended that a normal flower fertilizer be used, as this could burn the roots badly. This programme may be used for both types of dendrobium.

Repotting

This may be done every few years and at the start of the growing season (spring). If the flowers appear around the same time as the new growth (and this may well happen), wait until the flowers are over and then repot. As with cymbidiums, do not overpot – dendrobium roots are fine and sensitive, and plants prefer to be potted in as small a pot as possible.

Because they are epiphytic in nature, dendrobiums may be grown on blocks of wood or tree-fern fibre. As long as the humidity is kept up during their growing period they will soon attach themselves to the wood and produce many aerial roots (see illustration below). Place sphagnum moss around the roots and then firmly tie the plant and moss onto the wood. Someone once recommended using strips of ladies' tights – it works well and does not damage the plant. Try

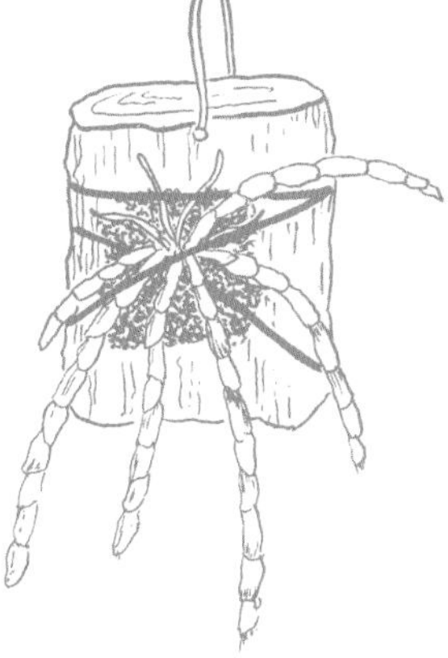

ABOVE Dendrobium growing on wood

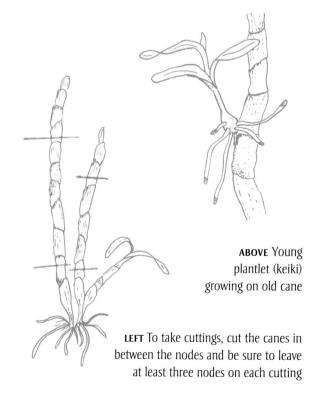

ABOVE *D. antennatum*

this method of growing a dendrobium as an alternative; it gives the plant a more natural look, particularly if you are able to hang it up in a conservatory.

Propagation

Propagating dendrobiums is very easy if they are well cultivated because they often produce young **plantlets (keikis)** along the old canes (see illustration on far right). These plantlets will eventually form their own bulbs with several roots. When the roots are more than 3cm (1¼in) long, the plantlets may be carefully removed from the mother plant and potted up.

An alternative form of propagation for sympodial orchids is to take cuttings. This may be done by removing a healthy, older, leafless cane (it is important to leave at least four or five canes on the plant) and cutting it into pieces of approximately 10–11cm (4–4½in) long. Cut the canes in between the nodes and be

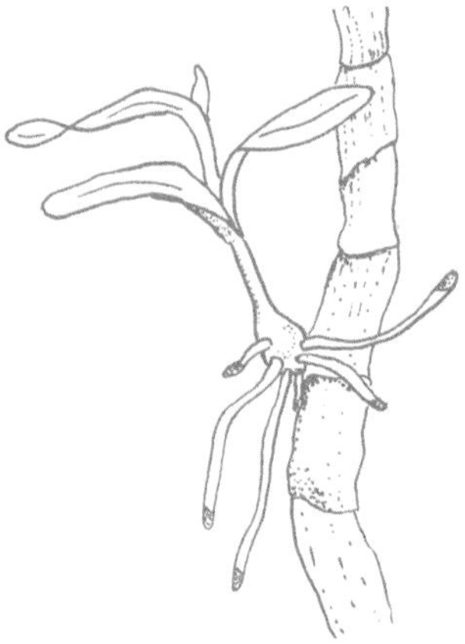

ABOVE Young plantlet (keiki) growing on old cane

LEFT To take cuttings, cut the canes in between the nodes and be sure to leave at least three nodes on each cutting

ABOVE *D. aggregatum: a* soft-caned species that is particularly good for beginners

sure to have at least three nodes on each cutting (see illustration on facing page). These pieces are then laid on a flat dish filled with moist sphagnum moss, with the cut ends just covered (see illustration below, right). To keep the moss moist, the dish may be put inside a clear plastic bag. In several weeks, new growths should appear; these, too, may be removed and potted up when large enough.

Pests and diseases

Like all orchids, dendrobiums may be kept pest-free, providing the greenhouse and surrounding areas are spotlessly clean. Under poor cultivation, they will be vulnerable to red spider mite and, when kept outdoors, snails! Snails love a nice, green, juicy pseudobulb and will munch a good chunk out of a cane.

Generally speaking, few pests and even fewer diseases can be expected when these orchids are kept in good condition.

Finally

It is advisable for beginners to start with the easier soft-caned species, such as *D. nobile*, *D. pierardii* (see page 35) and *D. aggregatum* (above). Once these have been successfully grown and have flowered, and if warmer and more humid conditions are available, you can move on to the hard-caned types (deciduous and evergreen). So, when buying a dendrobium, don't forget to ask what type it is before you settle on one or several.

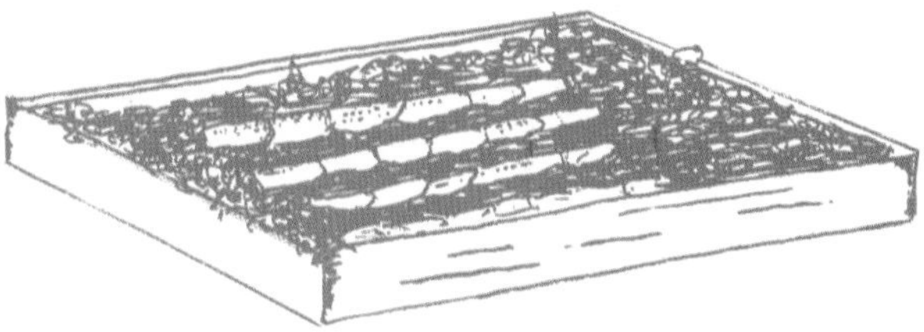

ABOVE Cut pseudobulbs placed on moist sphagnum moss

Phalaenopsis

From the Greek *phalaina* (meaning 'moth') and *opsis* (meaning 'appearance')

ABOVE *P.* 'Little Hal'

Phalaenopsis began its life as *Epidendrum amabilis*, through a **herbarium** specimen sent to the botanist Linnaeus in 1753, but was later established by the Dutch botanist Blume, who saw the specimen in flower and thought it resembled a moth in flight; it was therefore redesignated *Phalaenopsis amabilis*.

P. amabilis has pure white flowers, with a yellow and red-spotted throat and lip, and is a **variable** plant that flowers in the winter months (see page 44). It was once used extensively in hybridizing and has been crossed with just about every known phalaenopsis; it is the mother of most white hybrids today.

Habitat

Phalaenopsis is a truly tropical tree-dwelling (epiphytic) or rock-dwelling (lithophytic) orchid, found only in Asia (Indonesia, Malaysia, Myanmar and Taiwan). At least fifteen species and natural hybrids occur in the Philippines, where these tree dwellers, when in bloom, hover just like moths above the tropical vegetation. Some grow near the coast, others at high altitudes of 400m (1,300ft), but always in shady, humid places.

In nature, they live with a uniform temperature of up to 35°C (95°F) during the day and 25–26°C

(77–79°F) at night, with a steady, almost daily, rainfall during the monsoon that can reach as much as 240cm (100in) in a year, creating high humidity.

Characteristics

The flowers are magnificently, almost voluptuously, showy and irresistible, and some specimens, such as *P. schilleriana* from the Philippines, can have nearly 70 blooms on a single stem (see facing page). In their natural habitat they bloom continually, with the flowers lasting for months at a time and often producing a second flowering from the stem.

The foliage is distinctive, with huge, fleshy, ovate shapes up to 25cm (10in) long and 10cm (4in) wide, some marked with a silvery mottled effect, such as *P. stuartiana*. There are no pseudobulbs in this genus, so the fleshy leaves play an important role in storing food (which is mainly rotting vegetation) and water for the plant. One or two of the old leaves are shed each

ABOVE *P. amabilis*: the mother of most white hybrids today

ABOVE *P. schilleriana*: this stunning orchid can sometimes have as many as 70 blooms on a single stem

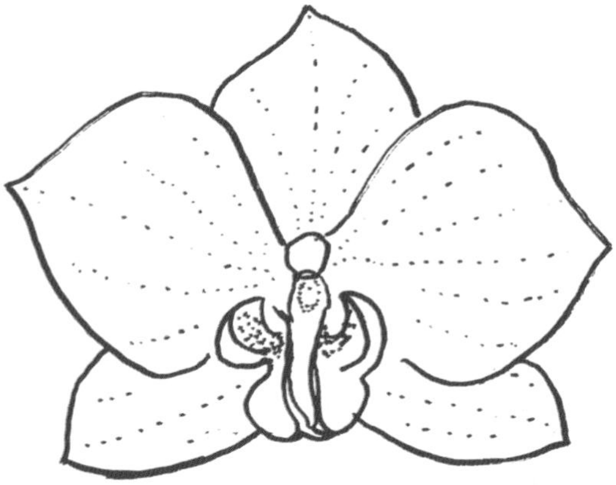

ABOVE Type I

LEFT *P. aphrodite*

ABOVE *P. stuartiana*

year, usually just after flowering has taken place, but are always replaced by new ones.

One remarkable feature of the phalaenopsis is its ability to produce roots that are often a metre (3ft) long, and not only collect moisture and food, but also cling firmly to their host for support.

Types of phalaenopsis

Phalaenopsis has two identifiable types. In Type I, the flowering stem may be quite long – 60cm (2ft) or more – and bearing as many as 15 or more blooms. The leaves are thick and fleshy, and elongate-elliptic and obtuse in shape. The flower petals are much broader than the sepals, and the lip produces two attractive curling

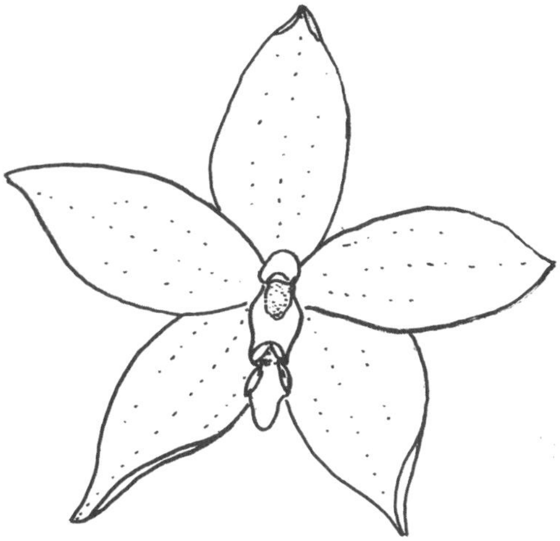

ABOVE Type II

centre lobes, and has **appendages**, or cirri (see illustration on page 46).

Species under this group are *P. parishii*, *P. aphrodite* (see page 46), *P. stuartiana* (see page 47), *P. schilleriana*, and *P. sanderiana* (a natural hybrid between *P. aphrodite*, which is white and *P. schilleriana*, which is mauve).

Type II has shorter stems and a different flowering habit to type I. Fewer blooms are produced at any one time on the flowering stem, but it continues to produce new flowers over several months. The flowers are smaller, the petals and sepals are equal in size, and the lip does not have appendages (see illustration on page 47).

Plants under this group are *P. cornu-cervi*, *P. leuddemanniana*, *P. equestris* (syn. *P. rosea* – used as a parent to produce *P. artemis*, the first man-made hybrid in 1892, see page 55), *P. mannii* (left), *P. amboinensis* and *P. intermedia* (a natural hybrid of *P. amabilis* and *P. equestris*).

Hybrids

In hybridizing, not only has phalaenopsis been crossed with phalaenopsis to create hundreds of new varieties, it has also been crossed with other **genera**, forming well-known cross-generic hybrids, such as asconopsis (phalaenopsis x ascocentrum), doritaenopsis (phalaenopsis x doritis), renanthopsis (phalaenopsis x renanthera), sarconopsis (phalaenopsis x sarchochilus), vandaenopsis (phalaenopsis x vanda), plus many, many more (see pages 50–51).

Conditions required for cultivation

When cultivation of phalaenopsis first took place, it seemed necessary to keep a greenhouse just for that species, but methods have improved since then and, many hybrids later, mature plants can now be grown successfully inside the house, even with central heating. If you think about it, both shade and warmth are readily available, plus a certain amount of humidity can be produced by placing pots on a tray of wet gravel, or misting with a fine spray. A conservatory full of plants is an ideal place, as long as there is enough shade for the orchid.

LEFT *P. mannii*

ABOVE X *Renanthopsis* Golden Lark

TOP LEFT X *Doritaenopsis* Elizabeth Castle Mont Millais

BOTTOM LEFT *Vandaenopsis*

Like most orchids, phalaenopsis begin new growth in spring. At this time, temperatures should be kept at approximately 20°C (68°F) during the day and no lower than 18°C (64°F) at night. Summer temperatures may be warmer (but no direct sun). During autumn, cooler temperatures of around 16°C (61°F) are a must to encourage flower formation.

Hybrid plants cared for under optimal conditions will produce flowers the whole year round, while species have a definite flowering period in spring and/or autumn.

So, although phalaenopsis flowers appear delicate and fragile, they are in fact not at all difficult to care for and, in spite of their origins, they are among the best indoor orchids available.

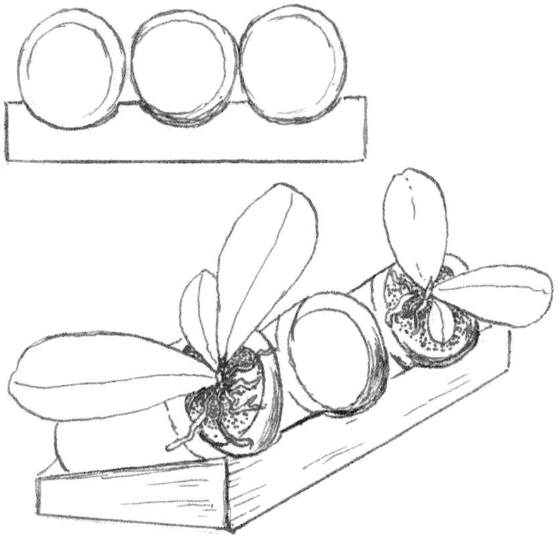

ABOVE Angled racks prevent water from accumulating in the leaves

RIGHT *P.* Tarragone x Marquess of Bath: just one of the many hundreds of phalaenopsis hybrids

Potting mix

Once again, a good, loose, air and water permeable mix is best. Think of this plant in nature attached to a tree: very little covers the root system, other than rotting vegetation, so it does not want to be 'stuffed' into a pot.

Use a mix of graded pine bark, some osmunda fibre, charcoal pieces and sphagnum moss, and keep the mix just damp until the roots are well established on a young plant.

If you have already been successful in growing phalaenopsis and are aware of their needs, try growing one on a piece of wood or tree-fern fibre, and attach the plant in the same way as you would with dendrobium (see *Dendrobium*, page 39, *Repotting*).

Watering and feeding

(a) Water

Plants must be kept evenly moist throughout the year, though they should be close to dry before the next watering occurs. They should not be allowed to dry out completely or become waterlogged. Usually, smaller plants require more frequent watering than larger, more mature plants, though this does depend on the compost: a large plant may require water twice a week during the summer, while a smaller plant may require water four to five times a week and once a week in winter.

Spray the leaves with a fine mist, but be sure that no residue water lodges in the centre: you should never allow water to accumulate in the centre or crown, as this will cause rot very quickly and could be fatal to the plant. In nature, these plants hang downwards, preventing

rainwater from accumulating in the new leaf. So, if you are going in for phalaenopsis in a big way, it would be worthwhile making a simple, angled rack to support the pots while laying them on their side (see illustrations on facing page).

(b) Feed

As mentioned earlier, phalaenopsis do not have pseudobulbs for food storage; therefore they require a good feeding programme. An orchid fertilizer of NPK 20:10:10 that has a higher nitrogen (N) content, should be applied every two weeks during the summer or warm weather and about once a month in cooler weather. Again, spray the roots and leaves with a fine, weak solution.

Repotting

Generally speaking, phalaenopsis should only be repotted when the mix deteriorates, when the drainage is poor, or when there is a root problem. This should be done during the growing season, but if problems occur before that, repot immediately, whatever the season.

Plants do better in pots which appear small for their size, but take care with roots that have attached themselves to the pot. Do not tear them away. Gently lever them off, taking care not to break the growing tip, which is bright green. It is better to break the pot than the roots.

After removing the plant, shake off the old compost and trim any brown, dead roots before placing the plant into a new container (preferably plastic as opposed to clay, which can dry out too quickly) with fresh compost and a little water.

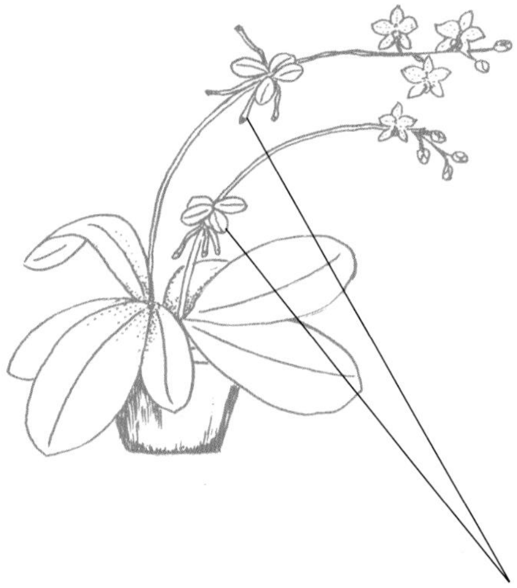

ABOVE A mature plant producing new plantlets (keikis)

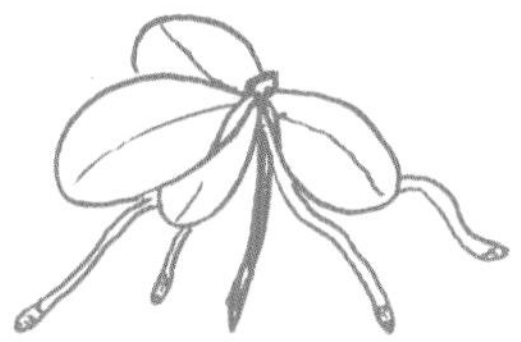

ABOVE A keiki ready for potting up

Propagation

Phalaenopsis species conveniently produce new plantlets (keikis) from the nodes of the flowering stem, particularly when the humidity is high (see illustration top right). Hybrids, however, do not produce them as easily. These keikis may be removed once several roots have formed (see illustration above) and then potted in the normal way. For this reason, it is important not to cut the flowering stem away after the last flower has dropped; leave it to see if: *a*. it will produce a secondary flowering stem, and *b*. it will produce these keikis.

Pests and diseases

(a) Pests

Phalaenopsis are often attacked by a false spider mite (*Brevipalpus russulus*), which causes small indentations or pitting on the top of the leaf surface. They are extremely difficult to see with the naked eye but are slightly red in colour and similar to red spider mite (*Tetranychus urticae*), which does not favour the phalaenopsis as much as other orchid genera. If they are not dealt with, a fungal infection could follow, resulting in leaf drop. A regular monthly spraying of an insecticide should control this, though humid conditions will also help deter these mites.

RIGHT *P. violacea*

ABOVE *P. equestris*

If your plants are in a greenhouse, be on the lookout for slugs and snails. Keeping your plants in hanging baskets or on a piece of wood can discourage them.

Allowing your plants to become too dry can also cause an attack of scale and aphids, so make sure you keep them well watered and inspect the underside of the foliage on a regular basis.

(b) Diseases

Overwatering or lack of air can cause fungal diseases in the leaves. Black rot loves high humidity with cool temperatures. It starts with purple/yellow blotches on the leaves and spreads quickly if it is not stopped.

Botrytis, which causes petal blight, generally appears in cool, damp weather with insufficient air circulation and will attack the older flowers.

Paphiopedilum

From Paphos – a city in Cyprus sacred to Venus – and Greek *pedilon* (meaning 'sandal')

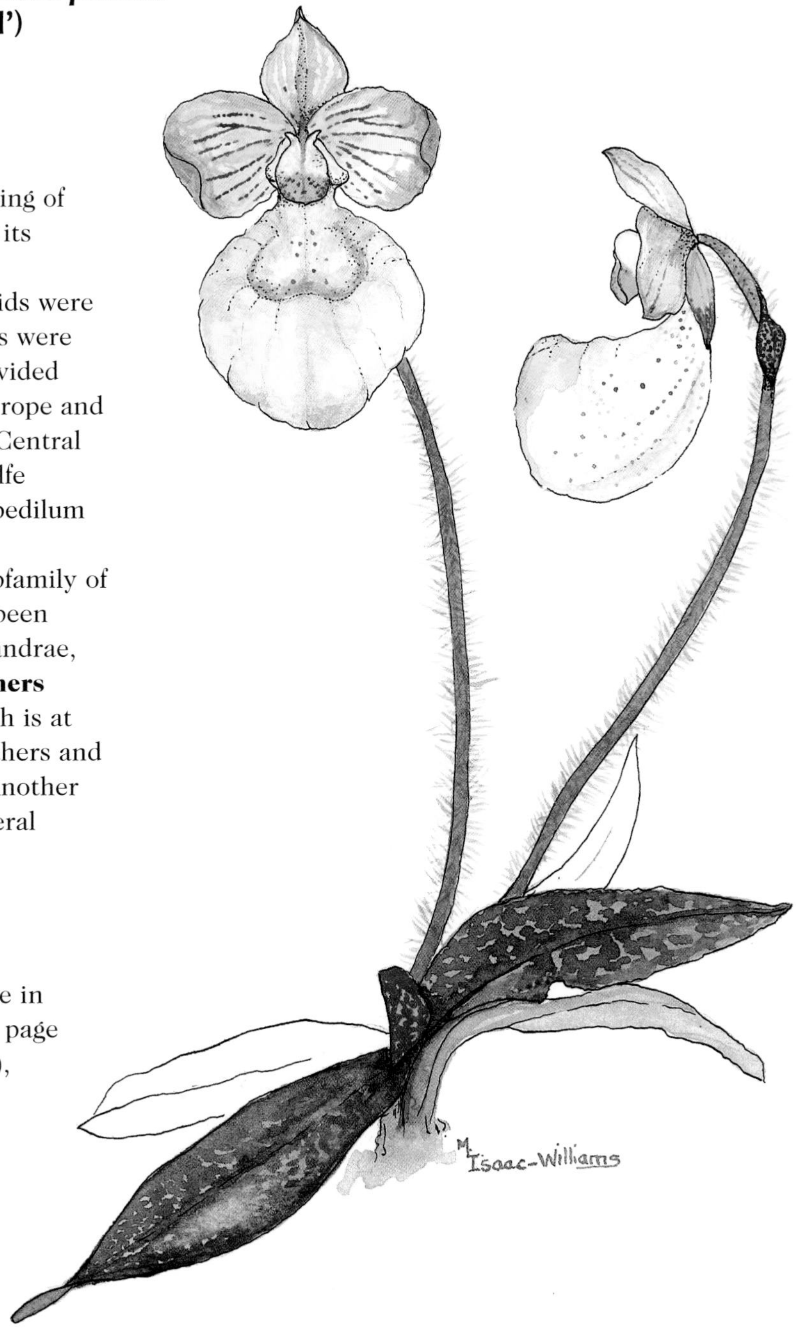

One of the most unusual and fascinating of orchids is the Slipper orchid, because of its unique pouch or slipper-like lip.

Prior to 1886, all 'Lady's Slipper' orchids were listed under cypripedium, but differences were discovered and now these orchids are divided into four groups: cypripedium Lindl. (Europe and North America), selenipedilum Rchb.f. (Central America and Brazil), phragmipedium Rolfe (Mexico, Ecuador and Peru) and paphiopedilum Pfitz. (tropical Asia).

All other orchids are placed in the subfamily of Monandrae, but the paphiopedilum has been placed in a separate subfamily called Diandrae, because the flowers have two fertile **anthers** instead of one, and the **staminode**, which is at the **apex** of the column, protects the anthers and stigma and is often hairy and wartlike. Another distinguishing feature is that the two lateral sepals are fused into one, forming the **synsepalum**, or ventral sepal.

History and popularity

The first paphiopedilum species to arrive in England, in 1819, was *P. venustum* (see page 66), followed by *P. insigne* (see page 60), which flowered in 1820. In 1823, *P.*

LEFT *P.* Winston Churchill x Vista

RIGHT *P. micanthrum*: unique among Asiatic paphiopedilums. The flower closely resembles cypripedium

ABOVE *P. philippinensis*: this unusual orchid may be found growing on limestone rock formations in the Philippines

javanicum appeared (see below) and 14 years later, in 1837, *P. purpuratum* (see page 60) arrived from Hong Kong.

They have remained one of the most popular orchids since they were first discovered and make excellent houseplants, with their amazing shape and combination of colours, veins, stripes, spots and hairs.

ABOVE *P. bougainvilleanum* 'Arawa'

Habitat

These unusual orchids are mainly terrestrial, although a few are known to be epiphytic. Their habitat ranges from shady, tropical forest floors to shaded mountain ravines and crevasses. There are about 60 species found in Asia, from the Himalayas and China to Indonesia, Borneo, New Guinea, the Philippines, Myanmar, Thailand and down the Pacific to the island of Bougainville, where the attractive green species *P. bougainvilleanum* (right) may be found.

In the Philippines, there are three endemic species: *P. haynaldianum* (see page 62), *P. philippinensis* (see facing page), and *P. argus*

ABOVE *P. javanicum* var. *virens*

ABOVE *P. purpuratum*

ABOVE *P. insigne*

(see page 63). The most unusual of the three is *P. philippinensis*, which originates from the southern island of Mindanao where it may be seen growing on limestone rock formations. It is characterized by its narrow and twisted petals, which are exceptionally long at approximately 15–21cm (6–8in).

Types of paphiopedilum

There are two main groups in this genus: *1.* species with leaves entirely green and usually found in the cooler mountainous regions of India and China up to 2,000m (6,500ft), and *2.* species with leaves that are tessellated, silvery-grey and green, and live in humid tropical areas such as Malaya, the Philippines and Borneo.

Both types have leaves that are formed in a **rosette** and, like the phalaenopsis, neither have pseudobulbs to store food and water. Each rosette usually produces a single flower stem, though species like *P. haynaldianum* and *P. lowii* produce between three and six flowers on a 30cm (1ft) long, hairy stem.

Hybrids

The first hybrid, *P. harrisianum*, was raised in England in 1869 and was the result of a cross between *P. villosum* and *P. barbatum* (both of which can be seen on page 65). The following year, *P. barbatum* and *P. fairieanum* (see page 64) were successfully crossed to form *P. vexillarium*. Between 1870 and 1900, 475 hybrids were created, and today there are more hybrids than there are species.

One very famous hybrid, 'Miller's Daughter', which won an award in 1971, has ancestry dating back to the 1880s, and had six species crossed to produce some of the 38 hybrids in its family tree. Now, 'Miller's Daughter' itself is being used as a hybrid parent (see facing page). It has very large

ABOVE *P.* Miller's Daughter 'Delilah'

dorsal sepals and petals, which are speckled with purple-red spots, and has a shiny white lip, resembling a small egg.

Conditions required for cultivation

The plain, green-leaved varieties require a different temperature to the tessellated types, but both may be housed in the same greenhouse, provided the temperature never falls below 14°C (57°F) at night (tessellated types prefer nearer 22°C (72°F) if they are grown on their own). This is because, in spite of their differences, the two types do adjust when grown together.

Proper shading and humidity must be provided during the summer when temperatures are higher (i.e. 25°C (77°F) during the day and no lower than 15°C (59°F) at night). During early autumn, after the shoots have finished forming, keep the plants cool for two to three weeks at night and sunny during the day.

As with phalaenopsis, paphiopedilums may be grown indoors where heating and shade are provided. Again, keep humidity up by standing the pots on wet gravel trays, or place the plants in a conservatory and mist around them, particularly during the summer. Remember, though, air movement is of extreme importance in the successful culture of these orchids.

If you are growing them inside the house, paphiopedilums should not be placed on a window sill that has full sunlight, as this will almost certainly cause leaf burn; in their natural habitat, paphiopedilums grow on jungle floors in the shade of other low-growing plants and require indirect sunlight. Do not give your plants an excessive amount of shade, though, as this will cause the leaves to fade through loss of chlorophyll, thus weakening the plant and making it vulnerable to fungal attacks; it will also contribute to a healthy plant's failure to flower.

ABOVE *P. haynaldianum*

Potting mix

After experimenting with various composts, most growers have finally settled on a potting medium that is well drained and 'open', but at the same time retains a certain amount of moisture. A layer of coarse charcoal or bark should be placed at the bottom of the pot to ensure good drainage, followed by a mix of medium fir bark chips, sphagnum peat moss, coarse shell grit and smaller pieces of charcoal. Alternatively, bark chips may be mixed with vermiculite, shell grit, charcoal and artificial granules of polystyrene and some moss; a pinch of limestone can also be added to reduce the acidity. If the plant is very small, a fine grade of fir bark should be used.

Watering and feeding

(a) Water

Watering will depend entirely on the conditions surrounding the paphiopedilums: if the humidity is high, as it may be in greenhouse conditions, the compost will stay moist longer and they will therefore require less frequent watering, particularly if they are in plastic pots; a good watering twice a week should be sufficient, as long as they are misted or sprayed daily. During the winter months, water moderately, and only during the middle of the day.

Do not allow water to settle in the centre of the plant, as this will damage buds and flowers. And it is always a good rule of thumb to allow the compost to *almost* dry out between waterings.

(b) Feed

During the summer months, fertilizer should be used fortnightly at approximately half the recommended strength. Immediately flowering ceases, a higher nitrogen feed should be given to promote plant growth; this may continue throughout the winter once a month.

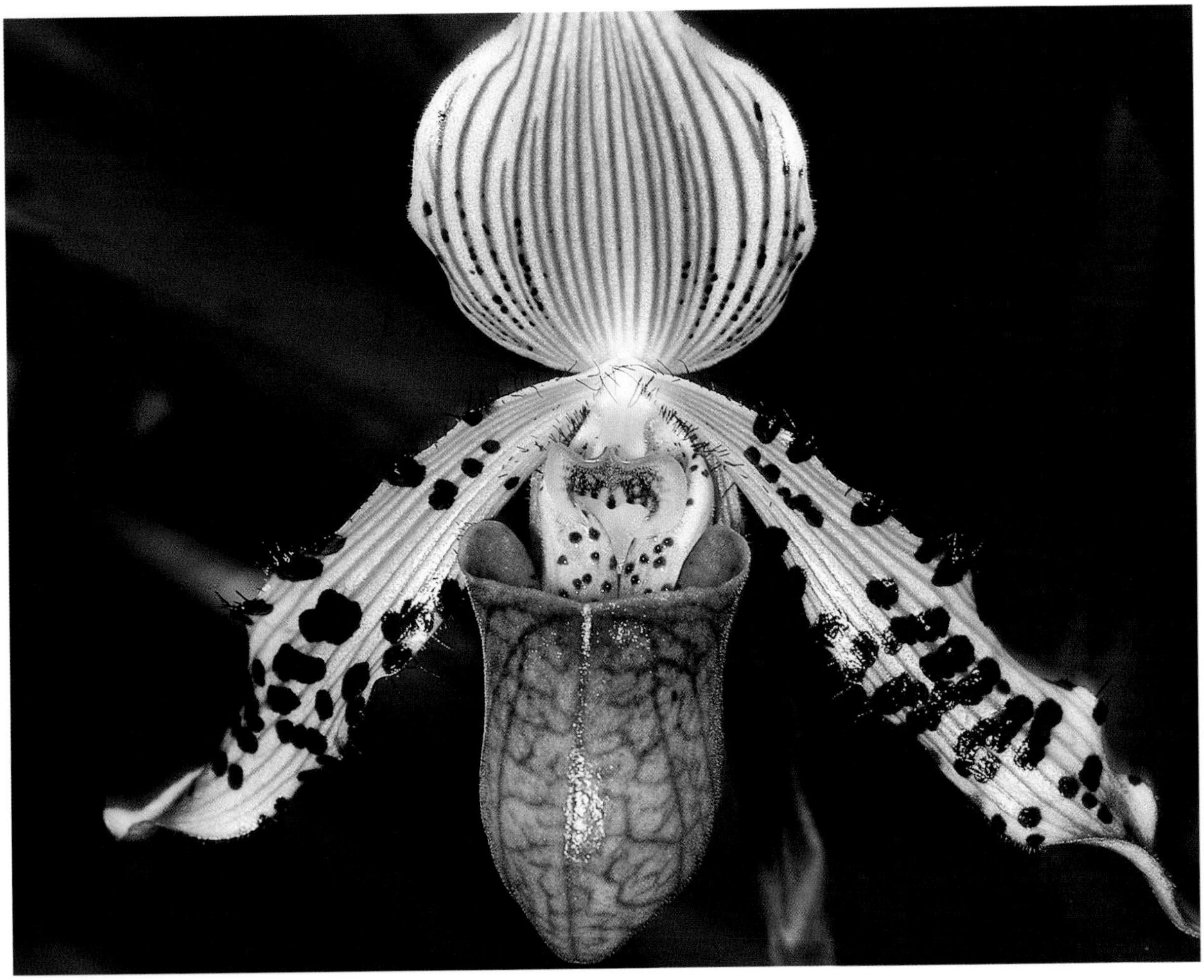

ABOVE *P. argus*

ABOVE *P. villosum* **RIGHT** *P. barbatum* 'Nigrum' **LEFT** *P. fairieanum*: *P. villosum* and *P. barbatum* were crossed to produce the first hybrid in 1869; the following year *P. barbatum* was crossed with *P. fairieanum*

A couple of months before the next flowering season is due to begin, a low nitrogen and high potassium and phosphorus mix must be used to initiate flower development. All mottled and plain-leaf species, which would normally grow in limestone areas (especially *P. fairieanum*), will benefit greatly from a small amount of lime or dolomite sprinkled on top of the compost once or twice a year.

Repotting

Mature plants should be repotted when they have outgrown their pot, when the growing medium has deteriorated or when it becomes hard and

ABOVE *P. venustum*: the first paphiopedilum species to arrive in England, in 1819

develops poor drainage. However, it does no harm to repot once every two years, in the spring when new growth begins, even if the plant is not **pot-bound**, as fresh growing medium is always beneficial.

Because of their meagre root system, young plants benefit greatly from being moved into as small a pot as possible. When doing this, check the old roots for rot. If you find any rotten roots, trim them off. Dusting the roots with a fungicide powder before repotting will prevent further problems. If the roots are not rotten, they need not be trimmed.

When repotting, take care not to bury any part of the plant above the roots or to pack the compost too tightly: this will prevent good drainage and cause rapid souring, followed by root rot. If the plant has very few or even no roots and appears unstable, place it on top of the compost and secure it to a small stake until a new root system takes hold.

Once the plant is repotted, water thoroughly

and then do not water again for at least a week: this will allow the roots to send out new tips to search for the water. Thereafter, water occasionally and, if the weather is hot, mist the leaves to prevent dehydration.

Propagation

It is not essential to divide Lady's Slippers, because they thrive well as a clump, giving a more spectacular show when flowering. In fact, some varieties are better left for many years without splitting, which can also weaken a plant. But, if you wish to do so, Lady's Slippers conveniently produce plantlets at the base of the main plant as it matures, and these may be divided at the time of repotting if it is a robust specimen and has at least two to three 'babies'.

Division must be done very carefully in order not to damage the entire plant. Sometimes you will find that once the compost is removed, the plantlets just fall away; at other times, they may still be reliant on the roots of the main plant and should not be separated.

Make sure that each plant has its own rootstock so that it is able to sustain itself once divided: if the bulk of the roots is left on the old plant, the new one will have very little to support it and will almost surely die. Gently prise the

ABOVE The attractive *P.* Jade Dragon

ABOVE *P.* Lippewunder

plants apart so that each one has as many roots as possible. Any old rotten roots should be removed, and the plant should be dusted with fungicide powder.

Pests and diseases

(a) Pests

This genus is relatively free from pests and diseases, as long as there are good growing conditions in the greenhouse. If your paphiopedilums are kept in a greenhouse on their own with the correct amount of humidity, there is little chance of red spider mite or whitefly appearing, as they do not like humidity. Do make sure, though, when buying a new plant that is pest-free, as you do not want it to cause an infestation among the rest of your plants.

Slugs and snails are always a threat and will cause havoc if not caught early. Sometimes the minute snails are dormant in sphagnum moss and will hatch once they are inside the warmth and humidity of a greenhouse. Prevention is always better than cure – a monthly watering with a slug killer should be sufficient.

(b) Diseases

Once again, these orchids are not prone to disease if the greenhouse is kept in tiptop

ABOVE *P. spicerianum*

condition. This may be achieved by spraying a good fungicide every couple of months. (Follow all instructions carefully and wear a face mask and goggles when spraying any type of horticultural chemical.)

Bud damp is probably one of the most common diseases, but this may be omitted if there is plenty of air circulation and careful watering. It is important that water is prevented from sitting in the growth centre where the bud emerges: if this occurs, rapid rotting of the buds will follow which, if left untreated, may develop into leaf rot. If this should happen, though, remove the leaf if the area is large, or cut out the section if the area is small, and then dust with a fungicide.

As long as the plants are in the right conditions, with good drainage and correct watering, there should be no other problems, not even root rot. However, if there were such a casualty, the plant should be removed from the potting medium and the diseased roots cut away. The plant should then be dusted with a fungicide and repotted in fresh compost. *Do not use the same pot*. Once repotted, the plant should be watered well and left for about ten days before beginning the same procedure as that of a normal repotted plant.

Pleione

Named after the mythological *Pleione* – mother of *Pleiades*

This genus, which has about 20 known species classed under the subtribe coelogyne, did not see immediate success in the orchid world; it was not until recent years that orchid growers began to take notice of the species and realize just how easy they are to grow.

Habitat

Being a mountain orchid, pleiones range from the Himalayas to Myanmar, Thailand, China and Taiwan, though most are found growing very close to the snowline in the Himalayas at altitudes of 1,000–3,500m (3,300–11,550ft) and in the cooler parts of China and Taiwan. Despite falling into the terrestrial category, pleiones will also grow on rocks and trees in their natural habitat.

ABOVE The beautifully marked *P. humilis*

LEFT *P.* zeus 'Weinstein'

It is in the Himalayas that the beautifully marked *Pleione humilis* (see page 71), *Pleione hookeriana* and *Pleione praecox* (see below) make their home, while *Pleione formosana* (see pages 73 and 75), with flowers ranging from pure white to a pale mauve and pink, is endemic to Taiwan (formerly known as Formosa, hence the species name). But the queen of the genus is *Pleione forrestii*, from south-west China and Myanmar. It is the only one of its colour, which varies from canary yellow to a bright orange-yellow, and has a fringed lip marked in red (see page 74).

Characteristics

Horticulturally, pleiones are unusual in that unlike other orchids with pseudobulbs they are not very large – the plant itself does not grow more than about 4cm (1–2in) off the ground. The flowering stem, however, can be as tall as 12cm (5in). In addition, they only last a year or two at the most.

The pseudobulbs are closely arranged, flask-shaped and often covered in small warts. The relatively large, showy flowers are similar in shape to coelogyne (see *Coelogyne*, pages 100–107). They appear either singly or in twos at the base of the pseudobulbs with the new shoots, and may reach 10cm (4in) across. They have rather narrow but free sepals and petals, the lip is tubular in shape, with the side lobes rolled over the column, and the mid-lobe is colourful and fringed (see illustration on facing page). The one or two long **plicate** leaves (up to 30cm/1ft) are deciduous and in most species drop before flowering begins.

When the flower is fully developed the leaves start to grow, which produce food for storage in the pseudobulbs. Once the flower has died away, a new pseudobulb develops at the base and the old pseudobulb gradually shrivels up. The pseudobulbs may then be stored in a cool, dry place for winter.

ABOVE *P. hookeriana*

ABOVE *P. praecox*

ABOVE *P. formosana:* pleiones have closely arranged, flask-shaped pseudobulbs and large, showy flowers, similar in shape to coelogyne

Conditions required for cultivation

Pleiones must be grown in cool conditions, such as a shady greenhouse, with temperatures of 10–13°C (50–55°F) at night and 16–21°C (61–70°F) during the day, and a stable humidity level of 70%. They also need bright but indirect, or filtered, sunlight.

During the summer months, the plants should be given good ventilation in a semi-shaded spot in order to keep the temperatures as far as possible to below 29°C (85°F).

In the autumn, after the leaves have dropped, pleiones require a rest period, during which time the compost must be kept just moist enough to sustain the pseudobulbs and prevent shrivelling.

Pleiones may be grown outdoors, but it is best if the garden bed is raised so that water runs off easily. Bulbs must be planted when the outside temperatures drop to 7°C (45°F). Although most of these orchids can withstand temperatures to 0°C (32°F), it would be wiser to take the plants indoors during the really cold winter months, when they are given a cold rest period after losing their leaves.

Potting mix

It is important that these orchids are grown in a fine but well-drained compost, made up of equal parts of bark, white sand, leaf mould and sphagnum moss. Care must be taken when planting that neither the pseudobulbs nor the new growth are buried in the compost; place the bulbs on top of the mix and gently nestle them in.

ABOVE *P. forrestii*: the only one of its colour, which varies from canary yellow to a bright orange-yellow

ABOVE *P. orizala*

Watering and feeding

(a) Water

After repotting, plants must be watered very carefully. For the first three or four weeks, water them sparingly until the new roots are well formed and actively growing; more water may then be given during active growth. At the same time, on every alternate watering a liquid feed at half the recommended strength may also be given until the flowers fade.

(b) Feed

Before late summer, it is a good idea to feed the plants a potash-based fertilizer to ripen the bulbs before the leaves fall again and the plants enter their dormant period once more.

Repotting and propagation

It is essential that repotting is carried out towards the end of the rest period in early winter, after flowering. At this time, the pseudobulbs can be separated, since they will have produced two new shoots during the **vegetative period**.

Pests and diseases

Fortunately, pleiones are almost pest- and disease-free. Just keep a watch on the ever-present snail lurking among the sphagnum moss!

Finally

This is an ideal orchid for amateurs or for first-time orchid growers. The pseudobulbs can usually be purchased from specialist nurseries, and plants may be grown very easily on north-facing window sills without winter heating.

ABOVE *P. formosana* 'Avalanche'

ABOVE *P. formosana*

jewel orchid

For some reason, 'jewels' have been given very little space in both orchid houses and books. Could it be because they do not possess the showy flowers of other genera? Admittedly, the flowers are quite small and normally white or grey-green, but in my opinion they produce the most beautiful leaves ever seen on any plant, and for that reason alone, they are well worth a place in an orchid collection.

Genera and habitat

Several genera spring to mind when mentioning jewel orchids: ludisia, or haemaria as it is also known (left), anoectochilus (see page 83), macodes (see page 78), goodyera (see page 79) and hetaeria – the latter two being less attractive to collectors than the others. Most may be found growing in the Himalayas, China, Myanmar, Malaysia, Hong Kong, Taiwan, Papua New Guinea and Australia, though others may be found in the Philippines, India, Sri Lanka, South and Central America and the West Indies. And while most of the species grow between altitudes of 500–1,800m (1,640–5,905ft), the growing conditions appear to be more important than the altitude.

Characteristics

The plants are usually single-stemmed and succulent, do not possess pseudobulbs, and are seldom more than 15cm (6in) tall without the inflorescence. The roots are produced at the nodes, and are spreading rather than deeply penetrating. The stem, for the main part, stays along the ground, terminating in an upright shoot

LEFT *Ludisia discolor*

ABOVE *Goodyera*

that carries the leaves, which are gemlike, velvety in appearance, and often bronze-green with golden-coppery veins shining in the sunlight. The flower spike appears from the crown of the leaves, bearing rather small flowers.

History

In the sixteenth and seventeenth centuries, Europeans believed in the 'Doctrine of Signatures', and according to this, jewel orchids were an effective medicine for snakebites. This belief derived from the fact that the leaves, with their network of coloured **venation**, resemble the markings on a snake and, like the snake, these plants are found creeping on forest floors among moist leaf litter in full shade or dappled sunlight (see page 83).

LUDISIA

Probably the easiest of jewel orchids to grow in a temperate climate, and certainly one that is available in orchid nurseries, is *Ludisia discolor*.

LEFT *Macodes petola*

There is only one species in the genus, which originated from the mountainous and lowland regions of China and Myanmar, down through Malaysia and Indonesia.

Characteristics

L. discolor is a very handsome, free-blooming dwarf orchid of the **variegated** foliage group. The thick, fleshy stems are purple-red and clothed with the most beautiful, dark, velvety green leaves, which are striped with fluorescent red-purple or golden veins and have an underside of purple-red (see page 80).

The flowering stem, which grows from the centre of the leaves up to 30cm (1ft) tall, appears in winter, clustered with waxy, white and yellow flowers that will last for months in perfection (see page 82). And although the flowers are small, they are attractive. The lip (**labellum**) of the flower is particularly interesting because, unusually, the yellow column and the lip twist in different directions, giving it a rather odd appearance (see page 81). Some growers like to pinch out the flower stems to encourage growth of the attractive

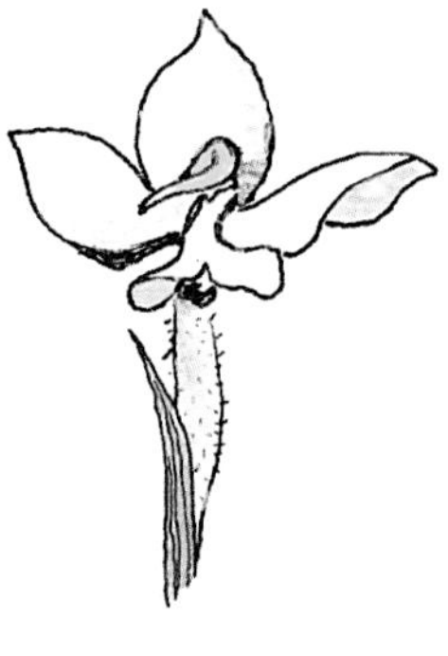

ABOVE Jewel orchids, such as this *Ludisia discolor,* usually have bronze-green leaves with golden-coppery veins and roots produced at the nodes

ABOVE The unusual flowers of *Ludisia discolor*

leaves, but since the flower is so interesting it seems a shame. But, of course, it is your choice.

Conditions required for cultivation

This orchid is very easy to keep in the house, as the light of a northern exposure is sufficient, although the leaf colour does remain more intense without direct sunlight. Temperatures may be kept at 16–18°C (61–64°F) and, providing there is normal air circulation, you should have no problems.

Potting mix

The mix may be made up of two parts coarse peat moss, two parts sandy loam, some fine bark, and one part vermiculite. Place a few small pebbles at the bottom of the dish for good drainage.

Watering and feeding

(a) Water

With good drainage, compost should be kept just evenly moist, but *not* soggy: if water is left standing around the roots, rot could occur. Watering once a week should be sufficient.

(b) Feed

During periods of active growth, a mild solution of orchid fertilizer may be given approximately once every three weeks. A balanced houseplant fertilizer will do equally well, providing it is given in half the recommended strength: excessive fertilizer can kill a plant and is not necessary if there is a high humus content in the potting mix.

Repotting

This need only be done when the plants become too crowded, or when the potting mix starts to deteriorate, preventing good drainage.

Propagation

The procedure is very simple: merely divide the creeping rhizomes by gently cutting through at a node or, if a long rhizome is available, cut into

LEFT *Ludisia discolor*

ABOVE Jewel orchids, like this *Anoectochilus yungianus*, may be found on forest floors among fallen leaves

several small sections and plant as normal. Make sure when using this method that the knife is sterilized and that the cut end is treated with a fungicide powder to protect it from a fungal attack.

Pests and diseases

(a) Pests

If your plant is indoors, and in the correct environment, there should be no problems at all. Outside, or in a greenhouse, the main worry is snails: they will chew their way through the rhizomes, creating holes or openings in which bacteria can soon take over.

(b) Diseases

The same applies for diseases as it does for pests: plants that are in the house in cool, airy conditions with correct watering should not be susceptible to any of the orchid diseases.

So, all in all, this is an extremely easy orchid to look after and certainly one that a real beginner could cope with, as long as the simple guidelines are followed.

ANOECTOCHILUS

From the Greek *anoektos* (meaning 'able to be opened') and *cheilos* (meaning 'lip').

ABOVE *Anoectochilus yungianus*

This small genus of shade-loving terrestrial herbs was first discovered in Java during the early 1820s by Blume, and concurrently in Nepal by Wallich. About 40 species are known to exist throughout Asia, with a large number found in Indonesia. There are also six species that are native to Malaysia, and several in Australia.

Characteristics

Like other jewel orchids, anoectochilus have slender, creeping rhizomes that send up rosettes of leaves, and, once again, there are no pseudobulbs for food storage. Leaves are a deep, velvety-green, or the most brilliant, metallic, emerald green, and sometimes a rich, warm brown or copper colour. Many are covered in a fine network of shining gold or silver veins that almost glow in the sunlight. The flowers are a little larger than *L. discolor* and more attractive, resembling a bird in flight (see illustration on facing page.

Species

Taiwan has two species of this orchid: *A. koshunensis*, which is endemic to the island, and *A. formosanus*, which may be found throughout most of the provinces of Taiwan, though, unfortunately, because of its use in some medicines and popularity with snails, it is becoming increasingly rare.

A. formosanus was first discovered in 1895 by Dr. Augustine Henry, who took it back to England where it was named *A. roxburghii* by R.A. Rolfe in 1903. In 1914, Hayata named the same species from the Taiwan University plant house as *A. formosanus*. In 1975, the confusion was finally sorted out when the Danish botanist Seidenfaden stated that *A. formosanus* was definitely not the same as *A. roxburghii*, although there were similarities, but if anything it was more like *A. siamensis*.

In Hong Kong, there is one species that was only discovered in the 1970s and bears the name *A. yungianus*, in honour of Dr. Yung, who was a college president of the Chinese University. The leaves of this orchid are brown-green and covered with a network of iridescent gold and copper veins, unlike *A. formosanus* which has white veins.

Australia has several species of jewel orchids, one of which lives in the wet tropics of northern Queensland and is named *Anoectochilus yatesiae*. Like *A. formosanus*, it, too, has dark green, velvety leaves that are tesselated with white veins. The flowers, however, are small and relatively unattractive.

ABOVE *Ludisia discolor variegatum*

Conditions required for cultivation

Anoectochilus should simply be treated in the same way as Ludisia, but with higher humidity.

Odontoglossum

From the Greek *odon* (meaning 'tooth') and Greek *glossa* (meaning 'tongue')

ABOVE x *O. lulii* 'Menuet'

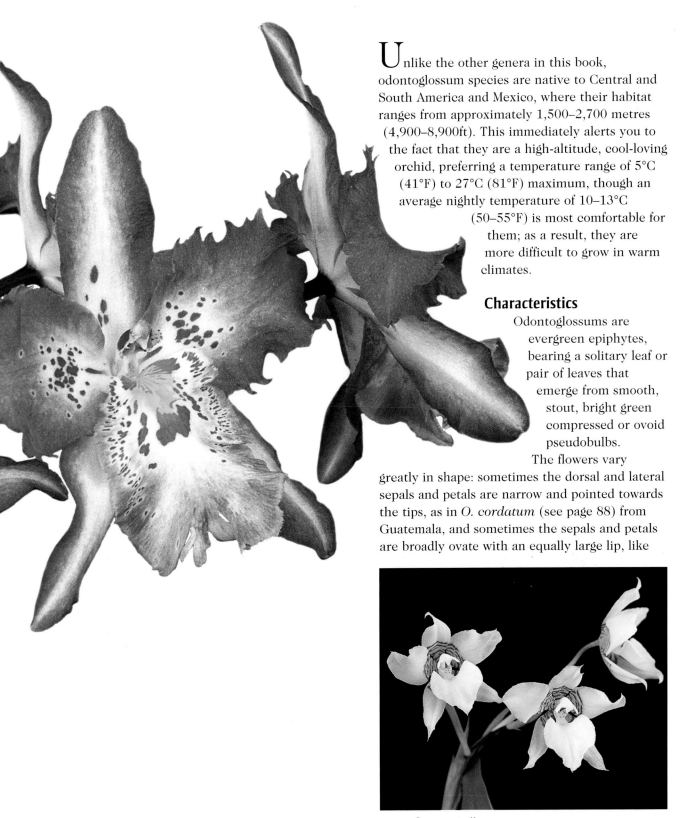

Unlike the other genera in this book, odontoglossum species are native to Central and South America and Mexico, where their habitat ranges from approximately 1,500–2,700 metres (4,900–8,900ft). This immediately alerts you to the fact that they are a high-altitude, cool-loving orchid, preferring a temperature range of 5°C (41°F) to 27°C (81°F) maximum, though an average nightly temperature of 10–13°C (50–55°F) is most comfortable for them; as a result, they are more difficult to grow in warm climates.

Characteristics

Odontoglossums are evergreen epiphytes, bearing a solitary leaf or pair of leaves that emerge from smooth, stout, bright green compressed or ovoid pseudobulbs.

The flowers vary greatly in shape: sometimes the dorsal and lateral sepals and petals are narrow and pointed towards the tips, as in *O. cordatum* (see page 88) from Guatemala, and sometimes the sepals and petals are broadly ovate with an equally large lip, like

ABOVE *O. cervantesii*

that of *O. cervantesii* from Mexico (see page 87). In others, such as *O. uro-skinneri*, the large, mauve lip is outsized in comparison to the sepals and petals.

The sepals and petals are often frilly, and the toothlike projections on the lip are characteristic of this genus. Colours vary from white to cream, yellow, brown, orange-brown, and bright magenta purple.

The length of the erect or slightly pendent flowering stems ranges from around 15cm (6in) to 120cm (47in), and may produce as many as twenty flowers at a time.

Species

There are over 400 species of odontoglossum, many of which are very robust, beautiful, and easily grown by beginners. *O. pulchellum* (see page 91), or Lily-of-the-Valley (so named because of its delightful fragrance), is a good species to begin with. Introduced into Great Britain in 1840 from Guatemala, *O. pulchellum* became an instant success because of the ease with which it could be cultivated. It is robust and grows up to 25cm (10in) tall, and has small, long-lasting, waxy, white, graceful flowers with a yellow blotch at the centre of the lip that bloom in winter and also in spring.

For a different type of odontoglossum, you cannot beat *O. grande*, or Clown Orchid (see illustration on page 90). It, too, is robust and grows up to 50cm (20in) tall and has large yellow flowers, with bright orange-brown markings. Originally from Guatemala, it is now one of the

ABOVE *O. cordatum*

ABOVE *O. crispum* 'Cristor'

ABOVE *O. grande* (Clown Orchid): one of the most widely grown odontoglossums

ABOVE *O. pulchellum* 'Bateman'

RIGHT *O. crispum*

BOTTOM RIGHT *O. harryanum:* discovered in 1886 and crossed with *O. crispum* in 1898 to produce the first hybrid

most widely grown orchids of this genus. It is also one of the few odontoglossums that has dark green leaves and tough-looking pseudobulbs.

Hybrids

Because of their beauty, and in spite of the huge range of species, it was not long before the first hybrid was created in 1898 by a Belgian. It was named *O. crispo-harryanum* and was produced through a cross between *O. crispum* (see above right), which is native to Colombia and has delicately large, broad, white-petalled flowers, with a touch of yellow and brown on the predominately white lip, and *O. harryanum* (right), which was discovered in 1886 and is also from Colombia. *O. harryanum* has a strikingly attractive flower, with coppery-brown sepals and petals and a large white lip, distinctively marked in bright lilac-mauve.

Odontoglossum crispum has since been used in a great many hybrids and is responsible for all the white hybrids with deep-coloured markings seen today, such as *O. stropheon* (see pages 92–93), which is the result of a cross between *O. Opheon* and *O.* 'Robert Strauss', but which also has grandparents in *O. crispum*, *O. pescatorei* and *O. harryanum*.

ABOVE *O.* Royal Wedding x triumphans: yellow was once an uncommon colour within this genus, but there are now several stunning hybrids in this colour

RIGHT *O. stropheon*

At one time, yellow was not a predominant colour in the species, but after crossing *O. luteo-purpureum* (pale yellow with heavy rust-brown markings), *O. harryanum* (coppery-brown, dappled with yellow), and *O. triumphans* (brown with yellow markings), there are now some stunning hybrids in golden and primrose yellow with occasional brown markings on the lip, such as *O.* 'Gold Cup'. This began the craze for hybridizing odontoglossums and, nowadays, there is an enormous range of hybrids in almost every conceivable colour.

Not only have many of the species been crossed within the genus, the genus itself has been crossed with other genera: oncidium (see *Introduction*, page 2) (forming the big genus odontocidium), cochlioda (forming odontioda, see page 94), and miltonia (forming vuylstekearas, see page 95). These **intergeneric** hybrids are able to tolerate higher daytime temperatures than odontoglossum alone, and are suitable for growing in warmer climates (such as the USA and Australia), and temperate climates that may have very hot summers.

Conditions required for cultivation

Spring is the time for new growth: new shoots and roots will emerge as the main plant comes out of winter rest. Minimum night temperatures

should be around 13°C (55°F), rising to approximately 20°C (68°F) during the day. Correct conditions at this time are important, and an abundance of healthy flowers will be the prize for such care.

Odontoglossums do like to be cool, so on warm summer afternoons, and if grown inside a greenhouse, they must be given heavy shade, humidity and good ventilation.

Temperatures during the day are critical to the plant: high temperatures will be damaging and scorch the leaves. A temperature of between 18–21°C (64–70°F) is congenial, with a minimum of 13°C (55°F) at night.

Humidity, too, is essential, and this may be maintained by damping down the floor or keeping pots on wet gravel trays. As in nature, continuous air movement is also important to keep the atmosphere fresh and buoyant, and high temperatures down.

Autumn, like spring, has favourable weather for growing conditions, and heating may not be necessary at this time. Again, minimum night temperatures should be around 13°C (55°F), rising to 20°C (68°F) during the day. If temperatures become higher during the day, damp down and make sure there is plenty of ventilation and shade. Generally, though, plants should be allowed maximum light throughout autumn. Plants do produce new shoots at this time, so it is important that they harden off before the long, cold, dark days of winter set in, otherwise they will be vulnerable to fungal attack.

Winter is the time when greenhouse conditions may deteriorate and, once again, it is stressed that great care must be taken with the watering of plants and with air ventilation. The minimum night temperature must be maintained: if it drops, keep the orchids on the dry side and lower the humidity.

ABOVE x *Odontioda* tigersette

ABOVE x *Odontioda* George McMahon

RIGHT *Vuylstekeara* Robin Pittman 'Trinity'

If you have space in the house, this is your answer to the winter months, especially since many species come into bloom during that time anyway. Odontoglossums thrive in normal household conditions and make a bright and welcome addition to homes. However, they do need to be placed in a cool room where there is air movement but no draughts, and light levels must be bright, so an easterly window or a shaded south-facing window in the house is ideal; a westerly exposure is too hot.

Potting mix

Since odontoglossums are epiphytic, they need open compost to provide good drainage. A

suggestion of seven parts graded bark, one part vermiculite and one part peat moss, with a little charcoal and sphagnum moss, have proved to be satisfactory. It must be open enough to drain well, but not so open that it cannot retain some moisture, as plants must not become dry during the growing season. Above all, these orchids dislike very wet or waterlogged compost, both of which would very quickly cause root rot.

Watering and feeding

(a) Water

Although some plants rest during the winter months, many of the species begin to flower; those that do will follow with their rest period, so allow plants to become dry. At this time, it is best to water every three to four weeks by using a spray bottle and directing the fine mist at the root system, while avoiding the rest of the plant. This will help to maintain pseudobulbs and prevent them from shrivelling.

In spring there should be an increase of water once the new growth appears, otherwise growth will slow down. Be careful, though, as too much water at this stage could cause rot on the young roots. Allow the compost to dry out between waterings, then, as soon as the mix is dry, give the plant water.

(b) Feed

Spring and summer is the time for a light feed every two to three weeks with a high nitrogen fertilizer (NPK 30:10:10) to encourage rapid growth during the active growing period, especially for plants in a bark-based potting mix. Dilute the fertilizer to half the recommended strength and spray around the roots and on the

ABOVE *Odontonia* Moliere 'Etoile'

ABOVE *Odontonia* Renée Ballerina

foliage. If the weather is continually dull, fertilize once every three weeks during that period.

From early autumn and until growth comes to a standstill, use a more balanced fertilizer to help initiate flower formation (e.g. NPK 10:20:20).

Please note that slow-release fertilizers should *not* be used because odontoglossums are not gross feeders; they would cause root burn.

Repotting

Either spring or autumn is the best time to repot, when plants are producing new roots and shoots. However, how often plants require repotting is variable and may depend on the state of the compost. Unless there is a problem, keep repotting to a minimum, as these orchids actually do not like being repotted too often – every two years should be sufficient for a mature plant (see illustration at top of page 98).

Before knocking the plant out of the old pot, check that you have a clean, suitable-size pot for your plant. The size, in this case, should be determined by the size of the plant and how many pseudobulbs it has, but it is better to use a smaller rather than a larger pot.

Remove some of the old back bulbs, but leave at least three bulbs, plus the new growth. Knock the plant out of the pot and remove all old compost. Old and dead pseudobulbs, plus dead roots (usually brown and soft), should be cut away and the new roots checked for any problems. If there is a sign of rot, spray with a fungicide before repotting.

ABOVE This plant needs repotting. Remove from pot

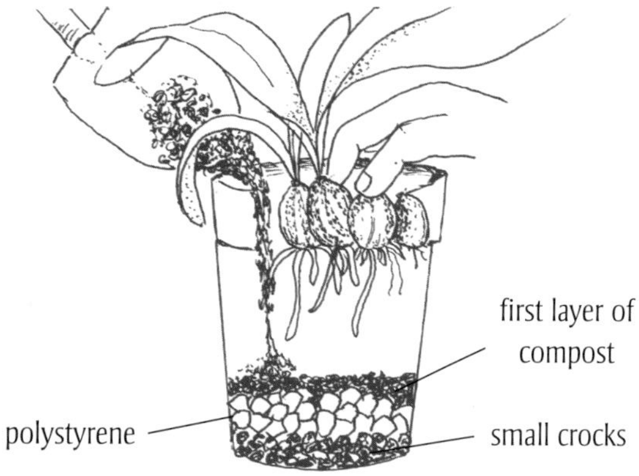

ABOVE Hold bulbs and fill pot with new compost

At the bottom of the pot, place either clean broken crock, small pebbles, or chunks of polystyrene, before covering with a thin layer of compost (see illustration on left). Hold the plant so that the base of the bulbs is level with the top of the compost and the old growth is almost flush with the side of the pot, as this allows space for new growth to move into the centre of the pot. Drop the compost around the plant and gently firm it down with your fingers. *Do not press too hard*. Then, add more mix and tap the pot occasionally to help settle the compost down.

Give the plant a good watering (although it is important not to overdo the watering at this stage) and place it in a shaded location. Provide some humidity, as this will help the roots to take in moisture, and then lightly water until the root system is well developed, which normally takes about six weeks. Follow with normal watering.

Propagation

Possibly one of the easiest forms of propagation is through the division of back bulbs. And although odontoglossums do not often throw out more than one shoot at a time, it is still the most effective way of propagating this orchid.

If the plant has more than two or three pseudobulbs behind the leading growth, then it may be divided up (see illustration below). This can be done a couple of months in advance of repotting by cutting the rhizome (using a sterilized knife that has preferably been passed through a flame) between the new growth and

ABOVE Potted plant showing space ahead for new growth

ABOVE Cut through the rhizome and remove old back bulbs and roots

the bulb behind. For instance, if you are planning to repot your main plant in April, cut the rhizome between the newest bulb and the bulb behind it two months before, and then do not disturb it until April. Meanwhile, new growth will have started on the bulbs and you will have a ready-made orchid for potting up separately from the rest of the plant. This method is particularly applicable to hybrids.

Some of the species of odontoglossum that produce more than a single new growth, such as *O. pulchellum*, may be propagated by division, which should be made up of at least two or three bulbs, plus new growth. If less bulbs are used, it could take nearly two years to produce flowers on the new plant. Once the new shoot appears, controlled watering is essential to prevent rot occurring.

Pests and diseases

(a) Pests

The most persistent of pests is the greenfly, followed in a lesser way by red spider mite, which will attack new shoots, soft leaves and flower buds if plants are not regularly sprayed with insecticide. Prepare the plants before they appear, as prevention is always better than cure.

As always, snails and slugs may be present and ready to demolish a nice, young, juicy shoot or flower. Use pellets on the floor of the greenhouse, or a molluscicide around the edges of pots. (Extreme care must be taken if children and animals are around.)

(b) Diseases

Provided there is plenty of airflow, the compost has not remained waterlogged or soggy during cold periods, and the greenhouse is kept clean, there should be no problems with fungal rot, and your odontoglossums will remain disease-free.

Finally

There is a wide range of odontoglossums, both species and hybrid, and new varieties are constantly being produced, so it may be difficult to decide on which plant to purchase. Go to a specialist nursery and talk to an expert, who can advise you where to begin. And remember: in spite of all that has been said regarding their care, they really are not at all difficult to look after.

ABOVE *O.* Violetta von Holm

Coelogyne

From the Greek *koilos* (meaning 'hollow') and *gyne* (meaning 'female')

Dr. Lindley, 'the father of modern orchidology', was the founder of this genus in 1825, using the species *C. cristata* as the type; it has been in great demand ever since. Coelogyne is of the subtribe coelogyneae, closely related to pleione and known to have more than 150 species, though there are possibly many more yet to be discovered.

Habitat

These evergreen epiphytes have a wide distribution, from the Himalayas, India and Sri Lanka to southern China and throughout Malaysia, the Philippines, Samoa, from the Fiji Islands to Vanuatu. Their habitat ranges from elevations of 300–3,030m (900–9,000ft), making them ideal for growing in very cool conditions.

ABOVE Pale yellow species, like *C. fimbriata*, are less common than white

LEFT *C. ochracea*

ABOVE *C. mooreana* 'Brockhurst' has densely arranged pseudobulbs

Coelogyne is the perfect orchid to grow in a conservatory without heating, and certainly one that would do well on a north-facing window in the house. It would also make a good companion to the *Dendrobium nobile* types mentioned earlier (see *Dendrobium*, pages 28–41).

Characteristics

The species vary a great deal within the genus, either producing densely arranged pseudobulbs (see above), ranging from approximately 2–14cm (1–5½in) with almost non-existent rhizomes, to well-spaced pseudobulbs attached to rhizomes as long as 15cm (6in). They may bear one to four broad, elliptic leaves on the bulb, which differ considerably in size and texture depending on the species.

Flowers may be single, few or many, small or medium-sized, appearing in gracefully curved or erect **racemes** from either the base of the pseudobulb or at the **apices** (see facing page), with the majority being white, although those from the Philippines are mainly slightly green or pale yellow.

The sepals are normally larger than the petals, subequal and often concave, and the petals are narrow and, in some species, almost **filiform**. The lip is trilobate and usually large, with two or more

ABOVE *C. stricta*

longitudinal **keels** with large, erect side lobes that almost completely envelop the column and gradually widen from the base of the lip.

Popularity

Coelogynes are among the easiest of all greenhouse orchids to grow, particularly *C. cristata*, which is frequently described as the 'beginner's orchid' (see below). It is a Himalayan species, and one quite often seen as a houseplant. It is popular the world over because of its ability in a cool climate to produce a mass of large, showy, white flowers with yellow keels on the lip. However, in spite of the many species and the ease with which coelogynes may be grown, it is uncommon to find many in an average collection, which is probably because so many of the plants produce small flowers that are purely of botanical interest.

A few of the more interesting species include: *C. sanderae* – a species from Myanmar that was first introduced into cultivation in 1893 and quite similar to *C. cristata* but is a smaller version; *C. corymbosa* (see facing page), *C. asperata* – indigenous to the southern Philippine Islands, Borneo, New Guinea and Sumatra (see facing page); *C. merrillii* – named after Dr. Merrill, the distinguished botanist; *C. pandurata* – one of the largest of all coelogynes with green flowers up to 10cm (4in) across and a lip partly covered in black hairs (see facing page); and *C. massangeana* (see page 106). Among those mentioned, two would appear to be particularly outstanding because of their size: *C. asperata*, which grows to a height of 1m (3–4ft) or more, with flowers of 3–5cm (1½–2in), and *C. pandurata*, described above.

Conditions required for cultivation

As mentioned earlier, many of the species require cool conditions, such as those from the Himalayas and the higher elevations of the Asian countries. However, a few require slightly warmer – but not hot – conditions, such as *C. asperata*, *C. pandurata*, *C. ochracea* (see page 100 and page 107) and *C. ovalis*. All species require high

ABOVE *C. cristata*: popular because of its mass of large, white, showy flowers

light levels, but not direct sunlight, as this will burn and damage the leaves, particularly if they are against a glass pane.

Potting mix

Whether plants are in pots or wooden baskets, coelogynes do well in a medium-grade fir bark, mixed with tree-fern fibre and some sphagnum moss with good drainage. Species may also be grown on slabs of wood or tree fern, since they are predominantly epiphytic.

Watering and feeding

(a) Water

During the growing months (spring and summer), the plants should be watered liberally. For the remainder of the year, though, it is advisable to keep them almost dry, particularly if they are in a moist greenhouse. If, however, you are keeping your plants inside a heated house but in a cool room, finely mist the plants with a spray every five to six weeks: this will be sufficient to prevent the plant from drying up and dying.

Species that require cool conditions (*C. cristata*, *C. pandurata*, and *C. ochracea*), and those that require medium conditions (*C. massangeana* and *C. mooreana*) must have a rest period after the new pseudobulbs have

ABOVE *C. corymbosa*

ABOVE *C. asperata*: a particularly tall species, growing to a height of 1m (3–4ft) or more

ABOVE *C. pandurata*: one of the largest species in this genus

ABOVE *C. massangeana*

ABOVE *C. leungiana*

matured. During this time, water must be kept to a minimum.

(b) Feed

Coelogynes are moderate feeders, requiring food from spring to late summer. Do not overfeed them, as this could burn their leaves, and do not feed them while they are resting (autumn to late winter). During spring and summer, provide them with a weak solution of an NPK fertilizer of 10:10:10, and every four to five weeks use clean, fresh water (rainwater if possible) to flush out any unused plant food from the compost, which, if allowed to build up, could harm the roots.

Repotting

Coelogynes dislike having their roots disturbed, so this should only be done when necessary, and only then after the rest period, when the new growth and new root shoots appear. It does not hurt the plant to stay in its pot for as long as possible, providing it gets all the nourishment it needs and the potting mix does not become stagnant or 'dead'. Allow the plants to grow into large specimens if all is well, and repot every two to three years.

Propagation

This may be done by splitting the pseudobulbs, unless the plant has become so large that it is taking up too much space in the greenhouse or conservatory, in which case it is better to leave it as a specimen plant.

Pests and diseases

There is very little to worry about here as long as the usual rules of hygiene are followed.

ABOVE *C. ochracea*: requires cool conditions

Finally

It is often suggested that *C. cristata*, which has been popular for many decades, is the 'beginner's orchid' and one with which to start a coelogyne collection. However, it is not entirely without its problems. These are not difficult to overcome, though: in autumn, a reasonably low temperature (almost to freezing point) is required to induce flowering; during summer, a cool temperature is necessary; and it is not suited to a centrally heated house.

ABOVE *C. cristata* var. *maxima*

Pests and diseases

Orchids, like other plants, can suffer from various pests and diseases. And it doesn't matter how perfect the growing conditions are, there is always the chance of a pest infestation and an outbreak of disease. Pests attack the young, healthy tissue in a plant, causing damage, which then gives access to fungal problems. Know your plants and look continually for signs that say: 'I am not very well – help me!' There will always be a reason why a plant is not quite up to par, and it is very often just a matter of looking at the underside of the leaves to find the answer.

It is the weaker plants that are mainly at risk, especially if their environment is incorrect (too much water, high humidity, not enough ventilation, or a combination of all three). If plants are suffering from this type of fungal problem, stop the watering, reduce the humidity, and ventilate the area as much as possible; spraying with a fungicide will also help.

If the problem is not fungal, it is more than likely to be a pest problem. Look closely at the underside of the leaves where most of these pests like to hide. If you do see something and don't know what it is, remove the leaf and take it to your garden centre where they should be able to identify it. Do not reach for the insecticide right away. Have a good look to see how small or large the problem is. If the pests are just starting, it may be possible to remove them by hand and gently clean the leaf with soapy water. But obviously, if it is at an advanced stage, then a more drastic solution is needed.

If it is necessary to spray an insecticide, read the instructions carefully, as these chemicals when administered too strongly will certainly damage the plants, but if they are not strong enough, they will be ineffective and will not eradicate the pests. Aside from this, it is never very desirable to pollute the atmosphere with harmful chemicals, so do use them sparingly.

An alternative to the use of chemicals would be to obtain some of the natural predators that control many of the pests commonly seen on orchids (see your local Department of Agriculture). However, if these are introduced, chemicals can no longer be used, as they would be as deadly to the predator as they would to the pest.

The problem may be reduced if when buying new plants you make sure they are healthy and have been propagated from an equally healthy stock: the healthier the plants, the more resistant they will be to disease. So, do ensure that new plants are not introduced to your collection until you are truly sure about this.

It is of extreme importance that the hygiene in the greenhouse is maintained at all times. It is advisable to wash down the walls and floors of the greenhouse on a regular basis to eradicate potential diseases and unwanted pests. Also, do not leave old pots and compost around, and remove all weeds, dead leaves and flowers, as these are a potential source of disease. Make sure the glass is cleaned of all algae, isolate or destroy any badly infected plants and, if overhead watering is used, make sure that no water is allowed to remain in the leaf axils – a good way to do this is to place your pots at a slight angle so that the plant is tilted downwards and residue water drips off.

Safe use of chemicals

Chemicals are dangerous and should be treated as such. Always wear gloves to prevent contact with the skin; always follow the manufacturer's instructions; mix only the amount required at the time; do not store the excess; and, finally, keep chemicals well out of reach of children and animals – the perfect solution is a locked cupboard.

Pests

1. Red Spider Mite and False Spider Mite

(*Tetranychus urticae* and *Brevipalpus russulus*)

(a) Description

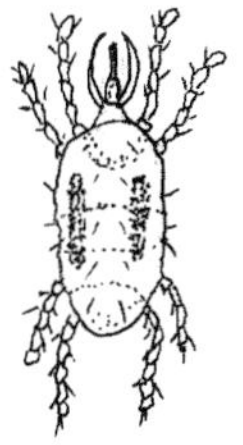

Red or yellow-green, less than 0.5mm (approx. 1/64in) in size, and almost invisible to the naked eye. Tap a leaf over a piece of white paper and they will fall off.

(b) Symptoms

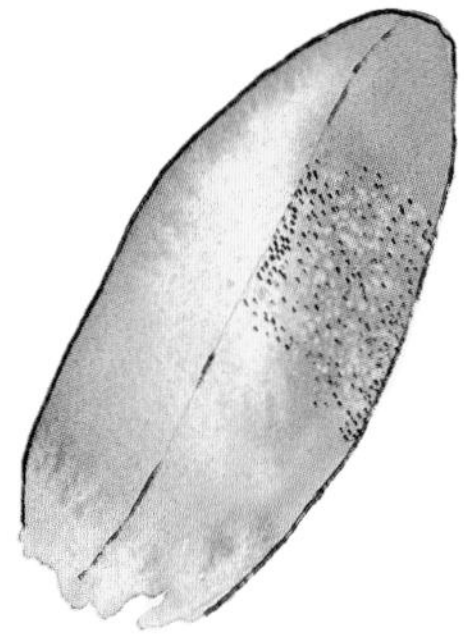

Normally, spider mites suck sap from the underside of the foliage, so leaves will appear pitted and mottled with white patches; if severe, leaves will turn yellow. Red spider mites will form fine white webs on the underside. Cymbidiums, dendrobiums and phalaenopsis are prone to attack.

(c) Remedy

Isolate the plant. For a minor problem, clean the foliage with warm, soapy water; heavy infestations should be sprayed with an insecticide. Most chemicals, however, will not eradicate the eggs, so it is important to spray badly infested plants at ten-day intervals to eradicate each new batch that hatches.

2. Scale

(a) Description

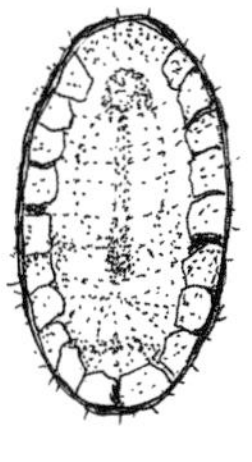

Scale is formed by sap-sucking insects of which there are two types in either brown, grey or white. Soft scale (*Coccus hesperidum*) is about 2–8mm (approx. 5/64–5/16in) long and produces honeydew. Hard scale (*Diaspis boisduvalii*) is less than 3mm (1/8in) long and does not produce honeydew, but does have a hard protective shell. They are clearly visible and remain in one spot.

(b) Symptoms

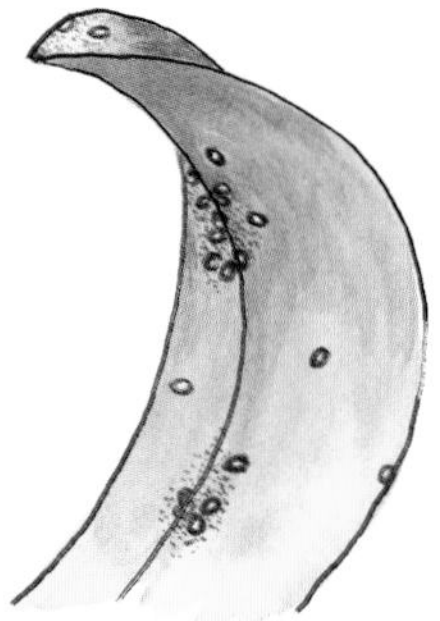

You will notice punctures, both on the top and underside of the foliage and pseudobulbs, often accompanied by a sooty mould. Plants will become stunted and leaves will turn yellow and drop. Paphiopedilums, cattleyas and cymbidiums are particularly prone.

(c) Remedy

For minor attacks, scale may be carefully removed with a small knife or wiped with cotton wool swabbed in a solution of half water and half alcohol or methylated spirits. Hard scale, with its protective shell, is almost completely resistant to chemical sprays, so a systemic insecticide (one that the plant absorbs) will make the plant toxic to these sap-sucking pests. It should be applied frequently over a period of two weeks.

3. Aphids

(a) Description

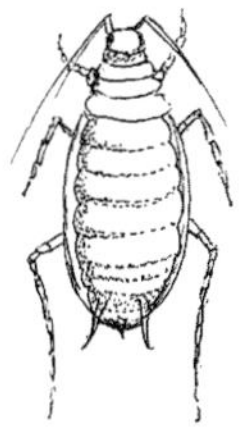

Aphids (*Cerataphis lataniae*) are disease-carrying, soft-bodied, flying insects, less than 3mm (1/8in) long, but quite visible. Their rounded bodies narrow towards the head; they secrete a sticky liquid known as honeydew that attracts ants and black fungus; and they are attracted to young growth and flower spikes with developing buds.

(b) Symptoms

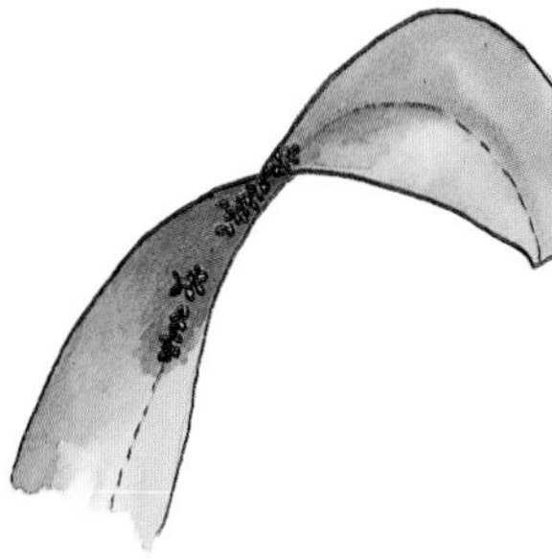

Developing buds often fail to open, or are malformed when they do, and leaves and stems appear stunted. Those that are most prone to attack are phalaenopsis, cattleyas and oncidiums.

(c) Remedy
Minor infestations may be removed by hand, and black fungus can be washed off with soapy water. Use an insecticide for a major infestation.

4. Mealybug

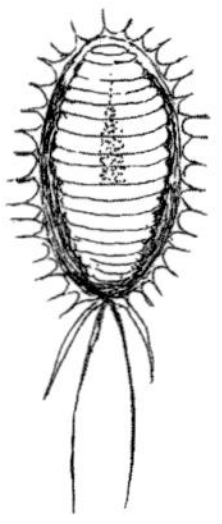

(a) Description
Mealybug (*Pseudococcus longispinus*) will attack most orchids, and is easily recognizable because it looks like white powdery blobs of cotton wool less than 6mm (¼in) long. Again, they are a sucking insect, and produce the sticky honeydew that attracts ants and black fungus. They may be found in the leaf axils, on new growth and on the underside of foliage.

(b) Symptoms
Plants may appear stunted or leaves may begin to look shrivelled. Dendrobiums, cattleyas and phalaenopsis are vulnerable.

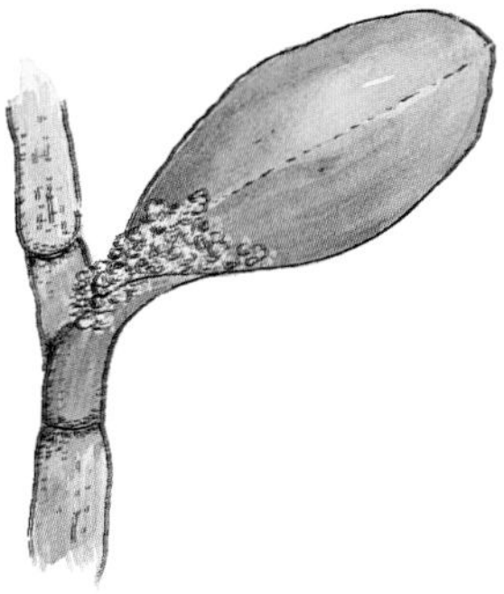

(c) Remedy
As with scale, use cotton wool swabs soaked in half water and half alcohol, or methylated spirits, or a mild liquid detergent. Heavier infestations will require an insecticide.

5. Slugs and snails

(a) Description
Both are molluscs, although slugs do not have shells like the snail. Snails normally range in size from 1.5 to 5cm (¾–2in) long and slugs can be up to 12.5cm (5in) in length. They normally hide during the day and emerge at night to do their damage on the foliage, roots, buds and flowers – they like it all!

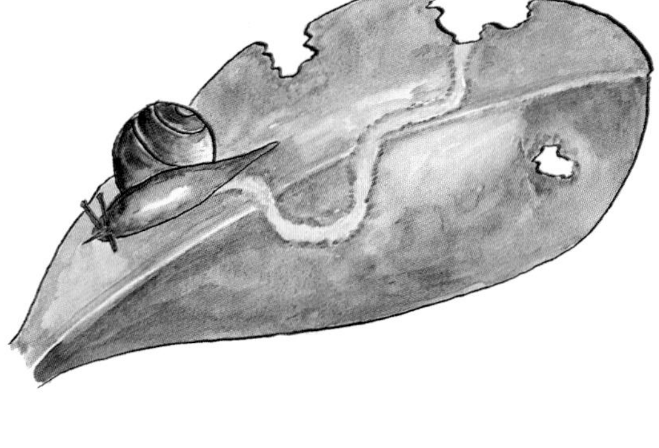

(b) Symptoms
Holes appear on the stems, buds are chewed right through, and roots and leaves are grazed of their chlorophyll. A slimy trail left behind is the telltale sign. All orchids are vulnerable.

(c) Remedy
Trap these pests at night with either slug bait in pellet form or a molluscicide.

Diseases

1. Black rot

(a) Description
Black rot appears as slightly purple blotches edged with yellow on the leaves and new shoots. It will either work its way downwards from the leaves, or upwards if it starts in the roots and pseudobulbs. It is caused by pythium and other types of fungi which favour cool temperatures, high humidity, and waterlogging. Phalaenopsis and cattleya-type orchids are most vulnerable.

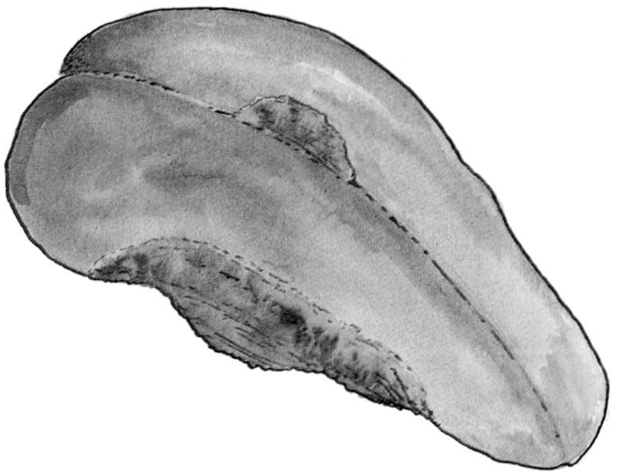

(b) Remedy
Cut out the infected part on the leaves with a clean, sharp knife and seal the cuts with a fungicide. If the entire orchid is affected, drench it with a fungicide, but if it is badly diseased, the whole plant should be destroyed. Make sure you *do not* use the knife on any other plant until it has been sterilized.

2. Petal Blight (Botrytis)

(a) Description
Botrytis is the other name used for this fungus, which begins as small brown circles with pink

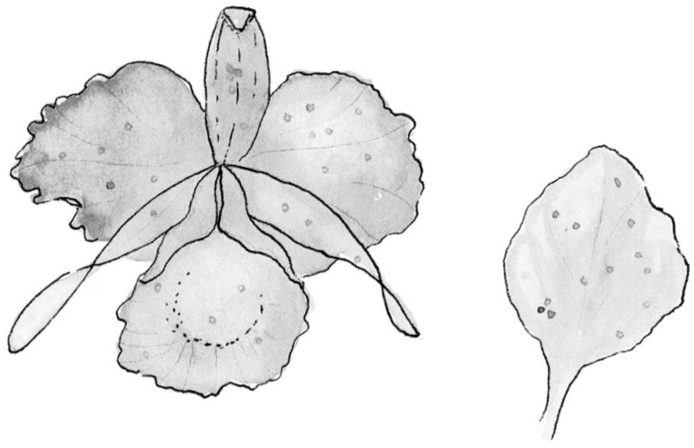

edges on the orchid's petals and sepals. The microscopic spores may be carried by water, insects or human hands, and will appear in a cool, damp atmosphere where there is little or no air circulation. Dendrobiums, vanda, phalaenopsis and cattleya-type orchids are all susceptible to this disease in poor conditions.

(b) Remedy
All infected flowers must be removed immediately and destroyed. The entire plant must be sprayed with a fungicide. Check that the humidity is not too high at night, when the temperatures are cooler. In autumn, a slight increase in temperature would help prevent the problem.

3. Leaf Spot

(a) Description
It is the fungi that thrive in high humidity that cause leaf spot. It may appear as either raised or sunken spots in brown or yellow, and will spread over the leaves very quickly. The leaves soon turn yellow or brown and die. It will almost certainly be fatal to young seedlings, but mature plants when treated quickly rarely succumb. Oncidiums, dendrobiums, vandas and phalaenopsis are vulnerable.

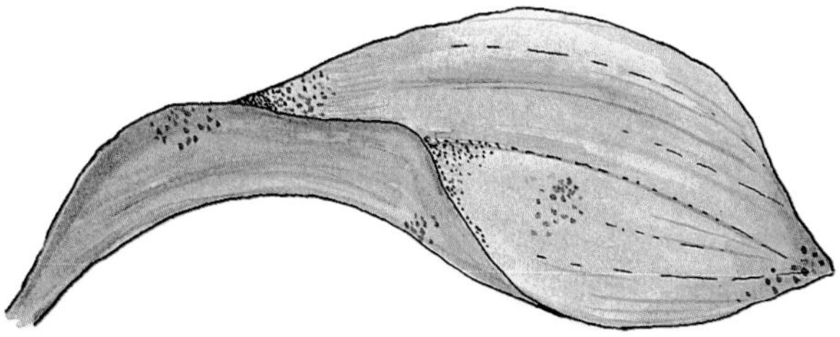

(b) Remedy
Diseased leaves must be cut off and cuts treated with a fungicide. Spray the plant once a week with a systemic fungicide, and also increase air circulation and reduce humidity.

4. Virus

(a) Description
For some reason, this virus has been misnamed 'cymbidium mosaic virus': misnamed because it will attack all orchids, not just the cymbidium. This disease spreads through the vascular system of the plants. It is highly infectious and may be transmitted very easily from tools, hands and aphids.

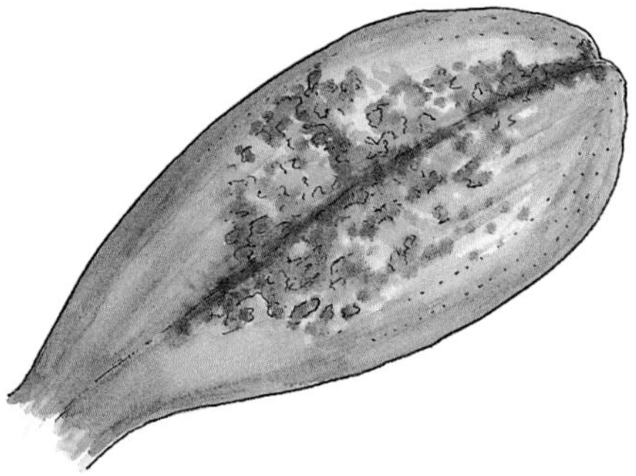

(b) Symptoms
Symptoms are discolouration of the leaves, which may be yellow, black or brown. As the disease advances, these patches become darker and sunken, mottled and streaky.

(c) Remedy
There is none! Destroy the infected plants to eliminate risk of spreading to other orchids. Make sure all cutting tools are sterilized before they are used again.

Finally

Most of the above may be avoided if the orchid environment is kept clean and free of old pots, composts, leaves, etc., there is good air circulation, and water is not allowed to collect in dishes or on the floor. On a hot day, you should water plants early, so that they will dry quickly, and, above all, check your plants on a weekly or, if you have time, daily basis. Use a magnifying glass to look for those pests that are invisible to the naked eye, for the sooner they are discovered, the easier they are to eliminate.

Glossary

Aerial roots roots that do not come into contact with the ground; they exist and grow in the air

Anther the part of the **stamen** containing the pollen

Anther cap a cap that covers the pollen

Apex the highest point

Apices plural of **apex**

Appendages subordinate parts of the plant

Axil the angle between a leaf or **bract** and the stem

Axis Main stem from which the secondary parts (branches, etc.) of the plant grow

Back bulb a **pseudobulb** that becomes dormant when the following year's pseudobulb takes over

Bract small, modified leaf on the **pedicel**

Cane the long jointed stem of the plant, also known as the **pseudobulb,** particularly with dendrobiums

Column the upright cylindrical structure that bears the **anther** and **stigma** in an orchid

Damping down wetting of floors and walls of glass houses
Deciduous a plant that drops its leaves at the end of the growing season
Disc the middle part of the **lip**
Division The process of dividing a single plant into one or more for **propagation**
Dorsal sepal the petal that stands upright behind the **lip**
Epiphyte a plant growing on another for support
Evergreen a plant that retains its foliage for at least a year
Filiform threadlike
Genera plural of **genus**
Genus a natural group of species having certain essential characteristics in common
Herbarium a collection of dried plants systematically arranged
Husk the dry outer covering of a **pseudobulb**
Hybrid a cross between two different **species** or hybrids
Inflorescence flower-bearing stalks
Intergeneric a cross between two or more **genera**
Keel the upright ridges on the **lip**
Keiki a **plantlet** produced on the main or flowering stem
Labellum (alternative name for **lip**)
Lamellae thin platelike structures
Lead newest growth
Leading bulb the newest bulb
Lip a modified petal, usually the most colourful
Lithophyte a plant that grows on rocks

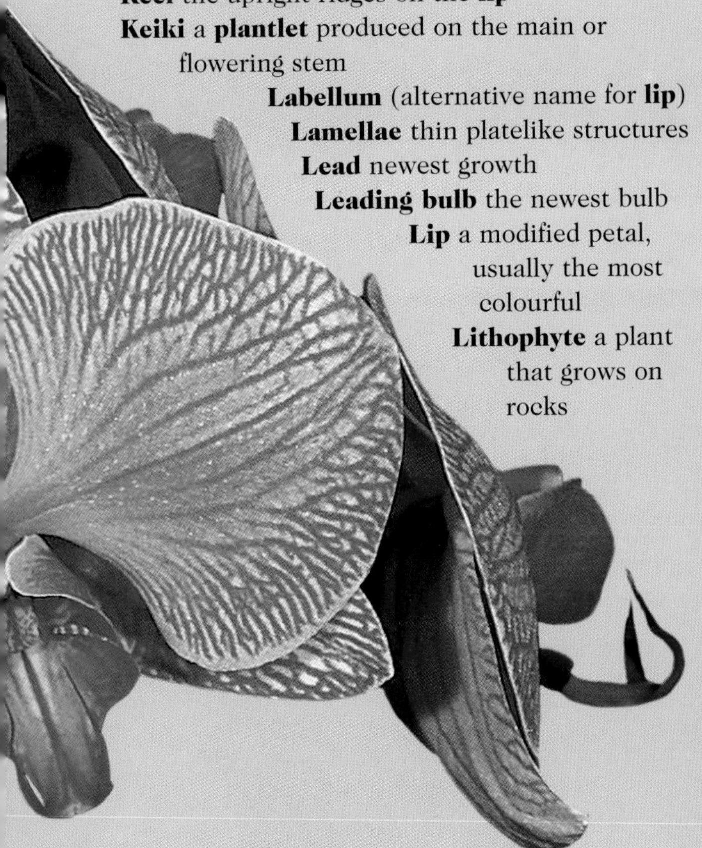

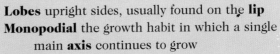

Lobes upright sides, usually found on the **lip**
Monopodial the growth habit in which a single main **axis** continues to grow
Monotypic a single **species** that constitutes a **genus**
Nodes joints in a stem
Overpot using too large a pot
Pedicel the short stem bearing a single flower
Pendent hanging
Pistil the female part of the flower, responsible for reproduction
Plantlets small plants
Plicate pleated
Pollinia pollen grains found in the **anther**
Pot-bound when a plant has outgrown its pot
Potted up a plant moved to the next size of pot
Propagating taking cuttings or growing a plant from seed
Pseudobulb rounded or thickened portion of stem, which stores food and water
Raceme flowers borne along the main stem
Rhizome creeping, horizontal, underground stem that joins the bulbs
Rosette a cluster of leaves around a short stem
Saprophyte lives on dead organic matter
Sepal the part of the flower that protects the developing bud
Species plants found growing in the wild
Spikes an **inflorescence** consisting of a **raceme** of flowers
Stamen the male part of the flower, bearing pollen
Staminode a sterile **stamen** or an organ growing in place of a stamen, as in the paphiopedilum
Stigma part of the **pistil** (female), which receives pollen
Sympodial having stems with limited apical (see **apex**) growth
Synsepalum lateral sepals fused into one single sepal (e.g. paphiopedilums)
Terrestrial found growing in the ground
Trilobate lip a lip with two lateral **lobes** and a mid-lobe
Variable capable of being different within the same **species**
Variegated variation of colour on foliage
Vegetative period the growing period of a plant
Venation arrangement of veins, as in a leaf

bibliography

Bennett, Keith S., *The Tropical Asiatic Slipper Orchid* (Angus & Robertson Publishers, 1984)

Bilton, Ray & Tibbs, Mike, *Orchids: an illustrated identifier and guide to cultivation* (Sandstone Books, 1998)

Black, Peter McKenzie, *The Complete Book of Orchid Growing* (Times Books, 1980)

Davis, Reg S. & Steiner, Mona Lisa, *Philippine Orchids* (Enrian Press, 1982)

Guest, Graham & Sue, *Cymbidiums* (Lane Print Group, 1992)

Isaac-Williams, Mark, *Introduction to the Orchids of Asia* (Angus & Robertson Publishers, 1988)

Kramer, Jack, *Botanical Orchids and How to Grow Them* (Garden Art Press, 1988)

Ritterhausen, Brian & Wilma, *Orchids* (Blandford Press, 1979)

Skelsey, Alice, *Orchids* (Time-Life Books, 1979)

Teo, Chris K.H. *Orchids for Tropical Gardens* (FEP International Pte. Ltd., 1979)

Wells, Diana, *100 flowers and how they got their names* (Workman Publishers, 1997)

Williams, Brian, *Orchids for Everyone* (Salamander Books Ltd, 1980)

About the author

Mark Isaac-Williams (BSc), a botanist and horticulturist, is a prominent authority on orchids. He developed his interest while working at Kadoorie Farm and Botanical Gardens in Hong Kong, for whom he travelled extensively throughout the Far East collecting orchids. In 1997 Mark left Hong Kong for Australia where he ran a wholesale nursery for three and a half years before coming to the UK where he now resides.

index

Note: page numbers in **bold** indicate illustrations

TITLES AVAILABLE FROM

GMC Publications

BOOKS

WOODCARVING

Beginning Woodcarving — *GMC Publications*
Carving Architectural Detail in Wood: The Classical Tradition — *Frederick Wilbur*
Carving Birds & Beasts — *GMC Publications*
Carving the Human Figure: Studies in Wood and Stone — *Dick Onians*
Carving Nature: Wildlife Studies in Wood — *Frank Fox-Wilson*
Carving on Turning — *Chris Pye*
Celtic Carved Lovespoons: 30 Patterns — *Sharon Littley & Clive Griffin*
Decorative Woodcarving (New Edition) — *Jeremy Williams*
Elements of Woodcarving — *Chris Pye*
Essential Woodcarving Techniques — *Dick Onians*
Figure Carving in Wood: Human and Animal Forms — *Sara Wilkinson*
Lettercarving in Wood: A Practical Course — *Chris Pye*
Relief Carving in Wood: A Practical Introduction — *Chris Pye*
Woodcarving for Beginners — *GMC Publications*
Woodcarving Made Easy — *Cynthia Rogers*
Woodcarving Tools, Materials & Equipment (New Edition in 2 vols.) — *Chris Pye*

WOODTURNING

Bowl Turning Techniques Masterclass — *Tony Boase*
Chris Child's Projects for Woodturners — *Chris Child*
Contemporary Turned Wood: New Perspectives in a Rich Tradition — *Ray Leier, Jan Peters & Kevin Wallace*
Decorating Turned Wood: The Maker's Eye — *Liz & Michael O'Donnell*
Green Woodwork — *Mike Abbott*
Intermediate Woodturning Projects — *GMC Publications*
Keith Rowley's Woodturning Projects — *Keith Rowley*
Making Screw Threads in Wood — *Fred Holder*
Segmented Turning: A Complete Guide — *Ron Hampton*
Turned Boxes: 50 Designs — *Chris Stott*
Turning Green Wood — *Michael O'Donnell*
Turning Pens and Pencils — *Kip Christensen & Rex Burningham*
Woodturning: Forms and Materials — *John Hunnex*
Woodturning: A Foundation Course (New Edition) — *Keith Rowley*
Woodturning: A Fresh Approach — *Robert Chapman*
Woodturning: An Individual Approach — *Dave Regester*
Woodturning: A Source Book of Shapes — *John Hunnex*
Woodturning Masterclass — *Tony Boase*
Woodturning Techniques — *GMC Publications*

WOODWORKING

Beginning Picture Marquetry — *Lawrence Threadgold*
Celtic Carved Lovespoons: 30 Patterns — *Sharon Littley & Clive Griffin*
Celtic Woodcraft — *Glenda Bennett*
Complete Woodfinishing (Revised Edition) — *Ian Hosker*
David Charlesworth's Furniture-Making Techniques — *David Charlesworth*
David Charlesworth's Furniture-Making Techniques – Volume 2 — *David Charlesworth*
Furniture-Making Projects for the Wood Craftsman — *GMC Publications*
Furniture-Making Techniques for the Wood Craftsman — *GMC Publications*
Furniture Projects with the Router — *Kevin Ley*
Furniture Restoration (Practical Crafts) — *Kevin Jan Bonner*
Furniture Restoration: A Professional at Work — *John Lloyd*
Furniture Restoration and Repair for Beginners — *Kevin Jan Bonner*
Furniture Restoration Workshop — *Kevin Jan Bonner*
Green Woodwork — *Mike Abbott*
Intarsia: 30 Patterns for the Scrollsaw — *John Everett*
Kevin Ley's Furniture Projects — *Kevin Ley*
Making Chairs and Tables – Volume 2 — *GMC Publications*
Making Classic English Furniture — *Paul Richardson*
Making Heirloom Boxes — *Peter Lloyd*
Making Screw Threads in Wood — *Fred Holder*
Making Woodwork Aids and Devices — *Robert Wearing*
Mastering the Router — *Ron Fox*
Pine Furniture Projects for the Home — *Dave Mackenzie*
Router Magic: Jigs, Fixtures and Tricks to Unleash your Router's Full Potential — *Bill Hylton*
Router Projects for the Home — *GMC Publications*
Router Tips & Techniques — *Robert Wearing*
Routing: A Workshop Handbook — *Anthony Bailey*
Routing for Beginners — *Anthony Bailey*
Sharpening: The Complete Guide — *Jim Kingshott*
Space-Saving Furniture Projects — *Dave Mackenzie*
Stickmaking: A Complete Course — *Andrew Jones & Clive George*
Stickmaking Handbook — *Andrew Jones & Clive George*
Storage Projects for the Router — *GMC Publications*
Veneering: A Complete Course — *Ian Hosker*
Veneering Handbook — *Ian Hosker*
Woodworking Techniques and Projects — *Anthony Bailey*
Woodworking with the Router: Professional Router Techniques any Woodworker can Use — *Bill Hylton & Fred Matlack*

UPHOLSTERY

Upholstery: A Complete Course (Revised Edition) — *David James*
Upholstery Restoration — *David James*
Upholstery Techniques & Projects — *David James*
Upholstery Tips and Hints — *David James*

TOYMAKING

Scrollsaw Toy Projects — *Ivor Carlyle*
Scrollsaw Toys for All Ages — *Ivor Carlyle*

DOLLS' HOUSES AND MINIATURES

1/12 Scale Character Figures for the Dolls' House — *James Carrington*
Americana in 1/12 Scale: 50 Authentic Projects — *Joanne Ogreenc & Mary Lou Santovec*
The Authentic Georgian Dolls' House — *Brian Long*
A Beginners' Guide to the Dolls' House Hobby — *Jean Nisbett*
Celtic, Medieval and Tudor Wall Hangings in 1/12 Scale Needlepoint — *Sandra Whitehead*
Creating Decorative Fabrics: Projects in 1/12 Scale — *Janet Storey*
Dolls' House Accessories, Fixtures and Fittings — *Andrea Barham*
Dolls' House Furniture: Easy-to-Make Projects in 1/12 Scale — *Freida Gray*

Dolls' House Makeovers *Jean Nisbett*

Dolls' House Window Treatments *Eve Harwood*

Edwardian-Style Hand-Knitted Fashion for 1/12 Scale Dolls *Yvonne Wakefield*

How to Make Your Dolls' House Special: Fresh Ideas for Decorating *Beryl Armstrong*

Making 1/12 Scale Wicker Furniture for the Dolls' House *Sheila Smith*

Making Miniature Chinese Rugs and Carpets *Carol Phillipson*

Making Miniature Food and Market Stalls *Angie Scarr*

Making Miniature Gardens *Freida Gray*

Making Miniature Oriental Rugs & Carpets *Meik & Ian McNaughton*

Making Miniatures: Projects for the 1/12 Scale Dolls' House *Christiane Berridge*

Making Period Dolls' House Accessories *Andrea Barham*

Making Tudor Dolls' Houses *Derek Rowbottom*

Making Upholstered Furniture in 1/12 Scale *Janet Storey*

Making Victorian Dolls' House Furniture *Patricia King*

Medieval and Tudor Needlecraft: Knights and Ladies in 1/12 Scale *Sandra Whitehead*

Miniature Bobbin Lace *Roz Snowden*

Miniature Crochet: Projects in 1/12 Scale *Roz Walters*

Miniature Embroidery for the Georgian Dolls' House *Pamela Warner*

Miniature Embroidery for the Tudor and Stuart Dolls' House *Pamela Warner*

Miniature Embroidery for the 20th-Century Dolls' House *Pamela Warner*

Miniature Embroidery for the Victorian Dolls' House *Pamela Warner*

Miniature Needlepoint Carpets *Janet Granger*

More Miniature Oriental Rugs & Carpets *Meik & Ian McNaughton*

Needlepoint 1/12 Scale: Design Collections for the Dolls' House *Felicity Price*

New Ideas for Miniature Bobbin Lace *Roz Snowden*

Patchwork Quilts for the Dolls' House: 20 Projects in 1/12 Scale *Sarah Williams*

Simple Country Furniture Projects in 1/12 Scale *Alison J. White*

Crafts

Bargello: A Fresh Approach to Florentine Embroidery *Brenda Day*

Beginning Picture Marquetry *Lawrence Threadgold*

Blackwork: A New Approach *Brenda Day*

Celtic Cross Stitch Designs *Carol Phillipson*

Celtic Knotwork Designs *Sheila Sturrock*

Celtic Knotwork Handbook *Sheila Sturrock*

Celtic Spirals and Other Designs *Sheila Sturrock*

Celtic Spirals Handbook *Sheila Sturrock*

Complete Pyrography *Stephen Poole*

Creating Made-to-Measure Knitwear: A Revolutionary Approach to Knitwear Design *Sylvia Wynn*

Creative Backstitch *Helen Hall*

Creative Log-Cabin Patchwork *Pauline Brown*

Creative Machine Knitting *GMC Publications*

The Creative Quilter: Techniques and Projects *Pauline Brown*

Cross-Stitch Designs from China *Carol Phillipson*

Cross-Stitch Floral Designs *Joanne Sanderson*

Decoration on Fabric: A Sourcebook of Ideas *Pauline Brown*

Decorative Beaded Purses *Enid Taylor*

Designing and Making Cards *Glennis Gilruth*

Designs for Pyrography and Other Crafts *Norma Gregory*

Dried Flowers: A Complete Guide *Lindy Bird*

Exotic Textiles in Needlepoint *Stella Knight*

Glass Engraving Pattern Book *John Everett*

Glass Painting *Emma Sedman*

Handcrafted Rugs *Sandra Hardy*

Hobby Ceramics: Techniques and Projects for Beginners *Patricia A. Waller*

How to Arrange Flowers: A Japanese Approach to English Design *Taeko Marvelly*

How to Make First-Class Cards *Debbie Brown*

An Introduction to Crewel Embroidery *Mave Glenny*

Machine-Knitted Babywear *Christine Eames*

Making Decorative Screens *Amanda Howes*

Making Fabergé-Style Eggs *Denise Hopper*

Making Fairies and Fantastical Creatures *Julie Sharp*

Making Hand-Sewn Boxes: Techniques and Projects *Jackie Woolsey*

Making Mini Cards, Gift Tags & Invitations *Glennis Gilruth*

Native American Bead Weaving *Lynne Garner*

New Ideas for Crochet: Stylish Projects for the Home *Darsha Capaldi*

Papercraft Projects for Special Occasions *Sine Chesterman*

Papermaking and Bookbinding: Coastal Inspirations *Joanne Kaar*

Patchwork for Beginners *Pauline Brown*

Pyrography Designs *Norma Gregory*

Rose Windows for Quilters *Angela Besley*

Silk Painting for Beginners *Jill Clay*

Sponge Painting *Ann Rooney*

Stained Glass: Techniques and Projects *Mary Shanahan*

Step-by-Step Pyrography Projects for the Solid Point Machine *Norma Gregory*

Stitched Cards and Gift Tags for Special Occasions *Carol Phillipson*

Tassel Making for Beginners *Enid Taylor*

Tatting Collage *Lindsay Rogers*

Tatting Patterns *Lyn Morton*

Temari: A Traditional Japanese Embroidery Technique *Margaret Ludlow*

Three-Dimensional Découpage: Innovative Projects for Beginners *Hilda Stokes*

Trompe l'Oeil: Techniques and Projects *Jan Lee Johnson*

Tudor Treasures to Embroider *Pamela Warner*

Wax Art *Hazel Marsh*

Gardening

Alpine Gardening *Chris & Valerie Wheeler*

Auriculas for Everyone: How to Grow and Show Perfect Plants *Mary Robinson*

Beginners' Guide to Herb Gardening *Yvonne Cuthbertson*

Beginners' Guide to Water Gardening *Graham Clarke*

Big Leaves for Exotic Effect *Stephen Griffith*

The Birdwatcher's Garden *Hazel & Pamela Johnson*

Companions to Clematis: Growing Clematis with Other Plants *Marigold Badcock*

Creating Contrast with Dark Plants *Freya Martin*

Creating Small Habitats for Wildlife in your Garden *Josie Briggs*

Exotics are Easy *GMC Publications*

Gardening with Hebes *Chris & Valerie Wheeler*

Gardening with Shrubs *Eric Sawford*

Gardening with Wild Plants *Julian Slatcher*

Growing Cacti and Other Succulents in the Conservatory and Indoors *Shirley-Anne Bell*

Growing Cacti and Other Succulents in the Garden *Shirley-Anne Bell*

Growing Successful Orchids in the Greenhouse and Conservatory *Mark Isaac-Williams*

Hardy Palms and Palm-Like Plants *Martyn Graham*

Hardy Perennials: A Beginner's Guide *Eric Sawford*

Hedges: Creating Screens and Edges *Averil Bedrich*

How to Attract Butterflies to your Garden *John & Maureen Tampion*

Marginal Plants *Bernard Sleeman*

Orchids are Easy: A Beginner's Guide to their Care and Cultivation *Tom Gilland*

Plant Alert: A Garden Guide for Parents *Catherine Collins*

Planting Plans for Your Garden *Jenny Shukman*

Sink and Container Gardening Using Dwarf Hardy Plants *Chris & Valerie Wheeler*

The Successful Conservatory and Growing Exotic Plants *Joan Phelan*
Success with Cuttings *Chris & Valerie Wheeler*
Success with Seeds *Chris & Valerie Wheeler*
Tropical Garden Style with Hardy Plants *Alan Hemsley*
Water Garden Projects: From Groundwork to Planting *Roger Sweetinburgh*

PHOTOGRAPHY

Close-Up on Insects *Robert Thompson*
Digital Enhancement for Landscape Photographers *Arjan Hoogendam & Herb Parkin*
Double Vision *Chris Weston & Nigel Hicks*
An Essential Guide to Bird Photography *Steve Young*
Field Guide to Bird Photography *Steve Young*
Field Guide to Landscape Photography *Peter Watson*
How to Photograph Pets *Nick Ridley*
In my Mind's Eye: Seeing in Black and White *Charlie Waite*
Life in the Wild: A Photographer's Year *Andy Rouse*
Light in the Landscape: A Photographer's Year *Peter Watson*
Outdoor Photography Portfolio *GMC Publications*
Photographers on Location with Charlie Waite *Charlie Waite*
Photographing Fungi in the Field *George McCarthy*
Photography for the Naturalist *Mark Lucock*
Photojournalism: An Essential Guide *David Herrod*
Professional Landscape and Environmental Photography: From 35mm to Large Format *Mark Lucock*
Rangefinder *Roger Hicks & Frances Schultz*
Underwater Photography *Paul Kay*
Viewpoints from Outdoor Photography *GMC Publications*
Where and How to Photograph Wildlife *Peter Evans*
Wildlife Photography Workshops *Steve & Ann Toon*

ART TECHNIQUES

Oil Paintings from your Garden: A Guide for Beginners *Rachel Shirley*

VIDEOS

Drop-in and Pinstuffed Seats *David James*
Stuffover Upholstery *David James*
Elliptical Turning *David Springett*
Woodturning Wizardry *David Springett*
Turning Between Centres: The Basics *Dennis White*
Turning Bowls *Dennis White*
Boxes, Goblets and Screw Threads *Dennis White*
Novelties and Projects *Dennis White*
Classic Profiles *Dennis White*
Twists and Advanced Turning *Dennis White*
Sharpening the Professional Way *Jim Kingshott*
Sharpening Turning & Carving Tools *Jim Kingshott*
Bowl Turning *John Jordan*
Hollow Turning *John Jordan*
Woodturning: A Foundation Course *Keith Rowley*
Carving a Figure: The Female Form *Ray Gonzalez*
The Router: A Beginner's Guide *Alan Goodsell*
The Scroll Saw: A Beginner's Guide *John Burke*

MAGAZINES

WOODTURNING ◆ WOODCARVING ◆
FURNITURE & CABINETMAKING
THE ROUTER ◆ NEW WOODWORKING ◆
THE DOLLS' HOUSE MAGAZINE
OUTDOOR PHOTOGRAPHY
BLACK & WHITE PHOTOGRAPHY
TRAVEL PHOTOGRAPHY
MACHINE KNITTING NEWS ◆ KNITTING
GUILD OF MASTER CRAFTSMEN NEWS

The above represents a full list of all titles currently published or scheduled to be published.
All are available direct from the Publishers or through bookshops, newsagents and specialist retailers.
To place an order, or to obtain a complete catalogue, contact:

GMC Publications,
Castle Place, 166 High Street, Lewes, East Sussex BN7 1XU United Kingdom
Tel: 01273 488005 Fax: 01273 402866
E-mail: pubs@thegmcgroup.com

Orders by credit card are accepted